Beyond Belief

Volume 1

DELLANNA W. O'BRIEN

Woman's Missionary Union
Birmingham, Alabama

Woman's Missionary Union
P. O. Box 830010
Birmingham, AL 35283-0010

For more information, visit our Web site at www.wmu.com or call 1-800-968-7301.

Dewey Decimal Classification: 231.7
Subject Headings: GOD (CHRISTIANITY)
                  MIRACLES—CHRISTIANITY
                  MISSIONARY STORIES

Cover design by Clay Allison

ISBN: 1-56309-286-7
W003102•0400•10M1

Contents

Prologue

"What did you learn in Sunday School, honey?"

"We learned about how Moses and the Israelites were being chased by Pharoah's army, and they came to the Red Sea. Since they couldn't get across, Moses called his team of engineers, who made this gigantic bridge so that all the people could cross to the other side."

"Now, sweetie, I don't believe that's what your teacher said."

"Well, no, Mom, it isn't. But if I told you what she really said, you sure wouldn't believe that!"

I, too, have found myself saying, "Incredible! This is almost beyond belief!" when reading portions of God's Word. The story of creation, the miracles Moses performed, the account of the young man raised from the dead at Zarephath, the virgin birth of Jesus, the miracles of physical healing, and most amazing of all, God's grace and mercy to everyone— all bring evidence that God is a God of miracles. His deeds seem almost too good to be true.

But is the age of miracles past? Do we simply read God's Word and marvel at the power once active among God's people but believe that it was for that era alone? Or is God's power still evident in the "beyond belief" events of today?

This book gives testimony to the proposition that God still acts in miraculous ways to accomplish His purposes. God continues to seek human instruments through which He can do His incredible works. May we all be challenged to make our lives available for His power to flow through us in ways too marvelous to believe—except through faith. We serve an incredibly mighty God. *That* you can believe!

Introduction

When our family served as missionaries in Indonesia, guests from the US were few. The distance and lack of good transportation made the trip to the central part of the island of Java difficult. A friend once rented a taxi for the long drive from Jakarta to our home in Semarang. At that time air-conditioning in cars was unheard of, and the tropical heat could be unbearable to newcomers. Our friend slowly extricated himself from the car and said, "When someone asks me where the ends of the earth is, I can tell them!"

Because we did not encounter many Western visitors, we were surprised one Sunday morning to see an American couple in the worship service of our church. When we introduced ourselves following the service, we discovered that they planned to stay in our area for several days, and we offered to show them around during their visit. We soon learned that they served as independent missionaries and lived in a nearby city.

After spending some time with the woman, I was impressed with her obvious sense of Christ's presence in her life. Her conversation was filled with expressions such as, "God just told me . . ." and "I felt God's leading me to . . ." She told me about going to the warehouse of a Christian relief agency seeking items needed by the Indonesian group they

3

served. She had a long list of the things they had requested—medicines, vitamins, food, and other necessities. The list also included lavender paint. She laughed as she explained that one of the missionaries' children wanted to paint her room lavender. "I told her that finding lavender paint was next to impossible. But guess what! They had one color of paint—lavender. God hears the prayers of His people, even the little ones. We found not only paint but everything else on the list. God provided it all."

Confession time. I have to admit that too often I had considered these details as outside God's area of interest. Too often I was prone to discount such facts as being just by chance or a matter of luck. Since then, I have discovered God's marvelous grace to His people far exceeds anything we could imagine. Just as He was active at creation, so He continues to work miracles in us and through us today.

To borrow the prayer of Paul for the Ephesians, I pray that your faith may be increased as you are reminded of God's miraculous power operative today as it was long ago: "I ask—ask the God of our Master, Jesus Christ, the God of glory—to make you intelligent and discerning in knowing him personally, your eyes focused and clear, so that you can see exactly what it is he is calling you to do, grasp the immensity of this glorious way of life he has for Christians, oh, the utter extravagance of his work in us who trust him—endless energy, boundless strength!" (Eph. 1:17–19 *The Message*).

And the Walls Came Tumbling Down

*P*erhaps no country on earth makes more extensive use of walls than Ireland, the Emerald Isle. With enclosures formed by trees or hedges, or more often by granite or limestone from the rich outcroppings throughout the land, these unique boundary markings bring color and personality to the lush green of the topography. Hugging the ribbonlike narrow roads, these walls often appear quite dangerous to motoring tourists, in spite of the fact that they are rarely ever more than a few feet high.

Following his fifth visit with his wife, Bonnie, to their beloved Ireland, my brother-in-law wrote the following description (Bonnie declares Chester thinks he discovered it!):

"We're driving an unfamiliar car, driver's seat on the right, stick shift on the left, and we're required to drive on the left—so the driver will be the first to be hit in the quite likely case of a collision. Those drivers who believe in the hereafter are most fortunate."

The visitor to Ireland finds his greatest driving challenge in negotiating the roads when meeting an oncoming car. Avoiding the car on one side and the wall on the other, the motorist finds the experience is rather like threading a needle with a very small eye. Fortunately, Bonnie and Chester escaped with no more damage than a hubcap crunched against a wall. In spite of the challenge of the walls, however, he says, "These were 14 of the most wonderful days of our lives."

The Chinese first built walls around houses and settlements, as well as political boundaries, more than 3,000 years ago. Feudal states warred for power and control, making walls necessary for protection and defense as early as the third century B.C. These first structures were made from dirt layered with stones and twigs and pressed into wooden frames, creating an early type of adobe, surprisingly strong and durable.

In the fifteenth and sixteenth centuries, the Chinese used stone to build the walls. The most famous of the Great Walls was built to fortify China's vast northern frontier against the Mongols. The ruins of this wall, a not-to-be-missed tourist attraction, have been partially restored near Beijing, and it is possible to climb and walk on this amazing structure. Spanning the rugged, mountainous terrain, the wall stretches about 1,500 miles and is at least 25 feet tall and 30 feet wide, allowing troops to march along its top. Watchtowers on the wall were built at regular intervals enabling an alarm to be sounded in case of danger. Today the massive fortification gives visitors the opportunity to test their physical stamina and, once having scaled the many steps to its heights, to see for miles around.

Two other walls serve as a time parenthesis around the Great Wall, one constructed before it, the other long after it. One was built before the beginning of a war, the other in war's aftermath. The purpose of one of these walls was to keep people out;

the other to keep people in. The destruction of each had elements of incredibility.

THE WALLS OF JERICHO

Moses was 120 years old when he died in Moab, but not before God had led him to the highest slopes of Pisgah on Mount Nebo. The climb, difficult for an old man, proved to be worth the effort, for there God gave him a glimpse of the land he had promised to Abraham, Isaac, and Jacob—and Moses. "I will give this land to your children and their children," He had told them. To Moses He added, "Moses, I have let you see it with your own eyes. But you will not go across the Jordan River to enter it" (Deut. 34:4, *paraphrase*). When Moses died, according to Scripture, God Himself buried him. For 30 days the people mourned his passing until the time for individual and corporate grief was over.

Then God began to mobilize His people for the conquest of the Promised Land. His first act related to the need for selecting a replacement for Moses. To His chosen Joshua He repeated promises of direction, victory, and His presence—if the Israelites would not turn away from Him (Josh. 1).

Joshua in turn put the Israelites on alert. "Three days from now you will go across the Jordan River. You will go in and take over the land your God is giving you."

The next days were a flurry of activity. For 40 years the people had been anticipating their entry into the Promised Land. In preparation for this long-awaited event, God demonstrated His power by once again parting the waters, this time of the Jordan River. Spies were sent out to survey the designated site of the first battle, Jericho. Joshua ordered the circumcision of the men, a rite neglected during the journey through the desert, as evidence of their willingness to be obedient. Before Joshua received the final orders for the conquest of Jericho, the people celebrated the Passover, a reminder of God's deliverance from Egypt and His desire to establish His people in a new land, a land flowing with milk and honey.

Sometime after the Passover feast, as Joshua was walking outside but near the city of Jericho, he met a stranger. "Friend or foe?" he asked (Josh. 5:13–15, *paraphrase*).

"Neither," the stranger replied. "I have come as the commander of the Lord's army." If Joshua had had any doubts, this announcement must have brought new resolve. The battle plan was not his, but the Lord's.

Jericho had to be the first military operation because of its position as the guardian fortress between the lower Jordan Valley and the central hill country of Canaan. Since the city presented a roadblock to further penetration, it was necessarily chosen as the initial object of Israel's advance.

The long-awaited day finally arrived. For six days, as instructed, the Israelites walked silently, wordlessly around the city of Jericho once. The only sound was formed by the blast of the trumpets by the priests. Military leaders of today would find it a strange strategy of war, but the Lord Himself had given Joshua strict instructions. "You shall march around the city, all the men of war going around the city once. Thus you shall do for six days" (Josh. 6:3, *paraphrase*).

The inhabitants of Jericho, expecting an attack, had closed and barred the city gates. All of Canaan had heard of the Israelite God Who parted the Red Sea and led its army in great victory. Rahab, a prostitute who had assisted the Israelite spies, confessed, "As soon as we heard it, our hearts melted, and there was no courage left in any of us, because of you" (Josh. 2:11 NRSV). Now Jericho's worst fears had materialized; they faced certain doom.

Confused, the citizens of Jericho watched for six days as the Israelites simply walked around the periphery of the city, just out of reach of the enemy's arrows. A vanguard of armed men led the march. Immediately behind them seven priests blew trumpets of rams' horns. Then came the ark of the covenant, symbolizing God's presence among them, and finally armed men brought up the ranks.

Because of Jericho's small size, comprising only eight or nine acres, the march took a mere 30 minutes. Imagine the surprise of the inhabitants of Jericho when their notorious assailants, after one revolution around the city walls, simply broke ranks and departed. Their amazement continued and their curiosity only grew when the Israelites repeated this action for six days.

Now the Israelites were ready for the final phase of their strategy. The armed vanguard stood in place; the priests waited, poised with trumpets ready. Men carried the ark of the covenant on their shoulders the specified distance of 1,000 feet behind. Then came the men of war, all marching silently around the city. Not a whisper escaped the lips of a single participant.

All proceeded as it had the preceding six days, but instead of stopping after one time around the city, the eerie march continued twice, three times, and on, until the group had made six complete revolutions. Following the seventh time around, the priests blew a long blast on the trumpets, and Joshua gave the signal, "Shout!" Every ounce of pent-up energy exploded in the release. It is difficult to imagine the discipline necessary for that week; throughout the six days, no one had uttered a sound. The order, "Shout," brought a primal scream we can only imagine.

Then the most amazing thing occurred. The walls fell down! The huge, heavy stones were tossed aside like children's building blocks. The Israelites were victorious because of God's presence with them. "So the Lord was with Joshua, and his fame was in all the land" (Josh. 6:27 NRSV).

If ever God's people needed evidence of His presence with them, this inexperienced, ragtag, erstwhile-followers-of-Jehovah army did. The miracle, which catapulted the Israelites into a new level of relationship with God, truly constitutes an awesome act of God—almost beyond belief.

BERLIN—ANOTHER DAY, ANOTHER CITY, ANOTHER WALL
Jericho's wall was shouted down around 1400 B.C. Some 3,300 years later, another significant wall claimed the world's attention. This wall was not built around a city, however, but divided one.

At the close of World War II in 1945, leaders from the US, Britain, and the Union of Soviet Socialist Republics (USSR) met at the Potsdam Conference to determine the disposition of their defeated foe, Germany. As a result of that conference, Germany, and Berlin the capital, were divided into four occupation zones, each ruled by one of the four powers (US, Britain, France, and USSR). The USSR was to command the eastern sector of the country as well as the eastern section of Berlin.

When the USSR began to establish Communist governments in Eastern Europe, the cold war began and tensions in Germany increased. Meanwhile, West Germany, with the aid of the Western powers, supported the free-market democracy and began to thrive economically.

Although East Germany held the distinction of most productive Communist nation between 1949 and 1961, its citizens were still aware that their standard of living fell substantially lower than that of their brothers and sisters in West Germany. During those years, at least 2.7 million people fled East Germany, most of them through West Berlin.

The Communist leaders realized that something had to be done to stem the hemorrhaging of East Germany's workforce. The answer? A wall! During the night of August 13, 1961, they began the building of a concrete wall, 12 feet high, and 103 miles long, of which 28 miles lay between two sides of Berlin. The only two openings of the Berlin Wall were two closely guarded crossing points, the more famous of which became known as Checkpoint Charlie.

The wall was reportedly built to protect Berlin from military aggression, but the tank traps and ditches along the eastern side of the wall revealed its real purpose, which was to keep the East Germans inside. In that, it was successful for the most part. More than 80 people died attempting to cross the border.

In 1984, following a meeting of the Baptist World Alliance General Council, my husband and I determined to visit East Berlin. Instead of entering the city through Checkpoint Charlie, we chose to go by subway. Before the war, during peace times, the subway had united the city, providing stations throughout the city. After the Potsdam Conference, however, East Berlin operated this mass-transit system. Only two stations, one in West Berlin, one in East Berlin, were used, and all the intermediate stops were closed. As we passed through the closed stations, the train slowed somewhat so that we could see the armed guards in the semidarkness, an eerie reminder of the enmity of the divided city.

At the checkpoint in East Berlin, guards made every attempt to intimidate us, from unfriendly, harsh commands, to leering at us over our passports, ostensibly to assure themselves we were the people pictured on the documents. It was the only time I felt grateful to look like my passport photo!

Once on the street, we were struck by the differences in East Berlin and West Berlin. Department store windows were sparsely filled with few items for sale, decidedly unlike the ample supply of goods in the West. We saw few people on the sidewalks; few cars in the street. Most noticeable of all, however, was the deafening silence. No talking, no laughter. Even in the restaurant where we ate, a hush lay heavily over the diners. The scene contrasted greatly with the joy, music, and entertainment of West Berlin, with its sidewalk mimes and musicians. We longed to meet Christian brothers and sisters who lived in the Communist territory and to encourage them. We returned to West Berlin with heavy hearts that night.

The next day, as we worshiped with West German Baptists, we remembered our Christian family in East Berlin who hungered to worship freely. Even then we joined our prayers with theirs that one day soon reunification would be a reality.

Erich Honecker, secretary general of East Germany from 1971 to 1989, continued to build that nation into a military and industrial powerhouse and to stifle internal political dissent as well. However, if Joshua had been mysteriously brought from the past to participate in the impending drama of this day, he would have had the priests warming up their trumpets. The time had come for the destruction of this wall.

Hungary symbolically sounded the charge by allowing East Germans to pass through their homeland to enter Austria and West Germany. Later that year it seemed apparent that East Germany teetered on the verge of collapse. On November 9, private citizens heard the whisper, "Shout!" Enthusiastic private citizens began to tear down whole sections of the wall without interference from government officials. West Berliners attacked the wall from the other side, until whole sections of the wall were demolished. The entire free world cheered at the sudden dismantling of Communism and the wall. World leaders were caught totally off guard by the precipitous action of both the East and West German populace.

Behind the scenes, however, Christian believers had quietly worked in preparation for the reunification of Germany. Theo Lehmann, a pastor in the regional church of Saxony, had been known for his strong faith in spite of Communist rule. He later had opportunity to see a review of his "crime" from his police file stating, "He believes everything written in the Bible and demands from young people total obedience to Jesus Christ."[1]

Lord Mayor of Dresden, Herbert Wagner, gave himself to the efforts for reunification of Germany for years. In greeting those attending the Baptist World Alliance General Council meeting in that city in 1999 he unveiled the steps resulting in freedom, stating:

"Ladies and gentlemen, the peaceful revolution ten years ago was not planned by a single political leader, and there was no visible general issuing orders in the background. . . . I am quite convinced;

miracles still happen today. We experienced it ourselves."

Wagner, as a member of a Group of 20, an informal band of Christian leaders, performed a great service for freedom. By his own definition the group was made up neither of elitists nor trained strategists. They did not claim status as heroes, for fear of the security police gripped their hearts. Marching under the banner of truth, justice, and love, however, these freedom leaders experienced a twentieth-century miracle.[2]

God heard the prayers of Christian leaders for the miracle that would bring Germany together. Like the Israelites at Jericho, they claimed the power of God Himself. Quietly, they worked behind the scenes, not planning massive military retaliation, but simply committing themselves to the strategy God would direct. When the time for action came, they could not take credit for the victory. God's powerful intervention in the affairs of His people once again amazed the world.

WALLS KEEPING OTHERS OUT

We who live in the United States have limited experience with walls. Prison walls that confine prisoners and walls intended to enhance the beauty of expensive homes and buildings form a short list of walled areas here. Even barricades that provide security for banks and other financial institutions, government buildings, and the like are constructed to diminish the exclusionary appearance.

We Americans pride ourselves on our free, open society. We can go anywhere, any time—almost. We do not erect walls to keep people out and certainly not to keep them in. We see ourselves generally as a wall-less people.

Why is it then that many nonbelievers are hesitant to enter our churches? Certainly no Christian would think of barring the entrance of our churches to anyone. Yet are non-Christians sometimes denied access by the invisible walls we unconsciously erect?

Some nonchurchgoers say they have never been invited. They will never perceive advertisements in the paper or on TV as an invitation. Furthermore, they would feel like fish out of water if they ever did attend a church service. They do not know the songs, cannot find the passages in the pew Bible, and dread the embarrassment of saying or doing something wrong. Moreover, many people fear an overzealous witness would coerce them to convert.

Many of our friends say they do not have the right clothes and cannot afford to buy them. They feel uncomfortable and out of place. All the Christians who attend, they say, appear to have it all together. Apparently, these saints have no questions, no problems, no doubts. If we could risk being vulnerable in acknowledging our deep-seated needs, others could see us, even devout Christians and faithful churchgoers, as we really are—seekers and pilgrims in the walk, trusting our heavenly Parent to teach, correct, and direct our steps. Perhaps our nonbelieving friends would find relevance for the church in their lives. Then we could begin to tear down the walls that keep some out.

WALLS WHICH KEEP US IN

Not only do we erect invisible barriers, for the most part quite unintentionally, which serve to keep people out of the church, but we likewise build walls which keep us inside the church, separated from the world. A number of years ago, we Baptists had what

16

was called "a six-point record system." In this self-evaluation we graded ourselves each week on actions designated as important in the Christian life. Such matters as being present at Sunday School, being on time, bringing our offering, studying our lesson in advance, reading our Bibles daily, and attending the worship service earned scores to determine our faithfulness for the week. A place to report any contacts made personally or by phone to invite others to church rounded out the report.

Thankfully, we discarded that system years ago. For too long it had indicated that as long as we attended Sunday School, arriving on time and having read the prescribed Bible lesson, we could consider ourselves honor roll Christians.

If God presented us with an evaluation system, what criteria would it contain? Certainly, it would involve church attendance, for His Word commands, "Let us not give up meeting together. . . . Instead, let us cheer each other up with words of hope" (Heb. 10:25 NIV). Christians find fellowship with other believers a necessary component in maintaining spiritual health. Genuine worship together, praising the wondrous acts of God and His love, joined with our prayers of intercession are seen as a primary purpose of the church.

In addition, God would place the study of His Word in a prominent position. How else can we know of His expectations for us if we know nothing of His standards? No doubt, God would place thoughtful, prayerful time spent devouring the teachings in the Bible high on His list.

Would God include acts other than gathering together important? Obviously, He would draw our attention to needs outside the walls of the building. As we worship, fellowship, and train to be the

Church in the world, our work is not complete until we have gone beyond the walls.

BREAKING DOWN WALLS IN OUR DAY

Acknowledging that many people in our country, in our day, have never been inside a church building stretches our imagination. In Christian America? How can that be? But the fact of the matter is we can never assume that any individual has ever heard of God's great salvation. It may be that the person who works beside you or lives next door has never read a Bible. Some would even say, "I've never known a Christian before."

Christians today must seek to share our faith with unbelievers in new and creative ways. It takes time and intention to develop relationships. How can we do this?

Find one person who does not know Christ—a co-worker, a neighbor, or an acquaintance—and get to know her. Spend time with her; learn about her family, her hopes, her concerns. Do not be afraid to share your own spiritual pilgrimage at appropriate times. Resist a judgmental attitude. Find ways, both tangible and intangible, to let her know you care. Tell her you pray for her.

When you feel comfortable inviting her to attend a worship service with you, determine beforehand the ways to make her more comfortable in her new experience. Sit with her, share your hymnbook and Bible with her. Give her an opportunity to relate her questions and feelings. Don't be afraid of not having the answer to theological questions. She will be more moved by your experience with Christ than with your biblical knowledge. Knowing certain verses that will be beneficial in leading her to Christ will be helpful.

After she accepts Christ as her Savior, stick by her side. Your job is not over yet. She will need you as never before to guide her and to disciple her. Do you fear not being competent to do this? Congratulations! You have just passed your first test. Only when we confess our inadequacies can God take charge. Only as we pray like we never have before can God destroy walls that divide.

It is only human nature to feel good with the familiar. We find comfort in being with friends of common beliefs and practices. We move freely in an environment where there are no surprises, no differences. Moving outside our comfort zones into the unknown entails great risk. In fact, most casual observers within or outside the church give highest commendation to the work within the confines of the church building. The more hours you spend there each week, the more highly you are praised.

Romans 12, however, issues a challenge to all believers to be faithful, even willing to sacrifice, as reasonable service. We cannot accept God's love without also embracing His mission. Jesus came to seek and to save the lost, to preach good news to the poor, to announce freedom for prisoners, and to bring sight to the blind. Where do we most often find the lost, the poor, the incarcerated, and the spiritually blind? Outside the walls of the Church.

So many areas of need pull us in every direction. Although we cannot respond to all, we must each claim the need that God places on our hearts. Pray first that God will give you direction. Then say, "If I had no fear in my heart, what difference could I make in someone's life? If I made time for a ministry, what would it be?" God will give you courage to risk and in so doing know the supreme joy in His service.

The great God has sounded the charge in life's most significant engagement. Walls must be broken down to claim entrance into the Promised Land for all who choose. Join the march around the world and be ready to lend your voice in the shout of salvation.

[1]Wendy Ryan, "New Hope in Dresden," *Baptist World,* October-December 1999.
[2]Herbert Wagner, Lord Mayor of Dresden, Germany, Welcome address, July 16, 1999, Dresden.

The Widow's Fight

*W*hat can compare with the awesome miracle of becoming a mother? Nothing can rival receiving that precious bundle into your arms and experiencing the wonder of it all. Psalm 139 beautifully expresses the marvel of birth. One or several birth experiences, the splendor never wanes. Each creative act claims its own unique joy.

The moment a mother inspects the head and face of her newborn and then opens up the blanket to be sure all the parts are there, she basks in the wonder, and is perhaps closest to God. Amazing! Toes, fingers, eyes, and ears, formed in miniature, function as God intends. Even when things go wrong, the Christian mother perceives that the heavenly Father loves this child far more than she does and will guide and bless.

The psalmist declares that even in the womb God has plans for each person. God's thoughts cradle the as yet unborn infant with love and intention.

"How precious to me are your thoughts, O God! How vast is the sum of them! Were I to count them, they would outnumber the grains of sand. When I awake, I am still with you" (Psalm 139:17–18 NIV).

Yes, no one can comprehend the miracle of birth.

But for some new mothers, fears, helplessness, and desperation crowd in on the happy event. Facing the awesome responsibility of rearing her child alone, she experiences a bittersweet joy. The mother in most of these instances will juggle multiple components in the family day after day. She worries about them when they are sick, helps with homework, disciplines, maintains schedules, and in the long run determines their future. At times she feels incompetent, stressed out, and without hope.

The situation grows more serious for the mother who is still a child herself. In 1994, 76 percent of teenagers who gave birth did so outside of marriage. Most experts tell us to expect an increase in teenage pregnancy in the next few years.

Some mothers find themselves alone because of divorce or the death of a husband. Lack of education and/or prior work experience means that the mother is unprepared to get or retain a job that will provide adequate income for herself and her children. Many of these women find themselves in the shelters for the homeless scattered across the country. The dreams of having a safe environment in which to live have been snatched from them.

Even in these dire experiences hope remains. God intervenes to bring peace and a future. We can find God's faithfulness in the pages of the Bible; we can know it from His mighty acts today.

ELISHA'S DRAMATIC SOLUTION

A woman during Old Testament times usually lived in subjection to father or husband. A woman's father gave her in marriage to another man who considered her not actually chattel property, but one totally under his authority. Normally, the woman had little or no choice in the selection of her husband, and he could divorce her freely and largely without reason. Fortunate the woman who was blessed with love and companionship in marriage, and, while not the cultural norm, Scripture contains many examples of devoted couples.

While marriage placed heavy burdens on most women in these times, widowhood heaped far more misfortune upon her. If a woman's husband died, she could receive no inheritance. A childless widow could return to her father if he were a priest and await marriage to a younger brother of her deceased husband. If the deceased husband had no brothers or if the financial means of the family could not be stretched to provide for the widow, she had no other resources.

Because of the harsh treatment of widows, prophets and others frequently condemned the injustices they endured. Interestingly, the Hebrew word for *widow* resembles the word for *mute,* perhaps referring to her lack of voice in providing for her own needs.

In 2 Kings 4 we read a most amazing story illustrating God's miraculous care of a powerless woman. When a man from the company of the prophets died, his wife sought out Elisha for help. The sons of prophets, not actually descendants of prophets, claimed membership in a guild or order established in the time of Samuel. Also called the company, or band, of prophets, they were recognized as prominent associates in the ministry of Elisha, who would no doubt have known and appreciated the work of the woman's deceased husband.

"My husband is dead. You know how much respect he had for the Lord. But he owed money to someone. And now that person is coming to take my two boys away. They will become slaves." (*Paraphrase.*) Claiming a debtor's children to work off a debt was common practice in those days. As far as the creditor was concerned, the law established his right; his conscience was free in this matter.

What could the woman do? It seemed apparent that she had run out of solutions. Elisha, however, would not give up so easily.

"How can I help you? Tell me. What do you have in your house?"

"I don't have anything there at all," she said. "All I have is a little olive oil."

Aha, thought Elisha. There *is* something!

"Go around to all of your neighbors. Ask them for empty jars. Get as many as you can. Then go inside your house. Shut the door behind you and your sons. Pour oil into all of the jars. As each jar is filled, put it over to one side," instructed Elisha.

Because of the widow's belief in Elisha or because of his commanding voice and demeanor, she hastened to do what he had said. After she and her sons had gathered the jars, they returned home, closing the door behind them. Carefully, not wanting to spill a drop, she poured the oil into the borrowed vessels until all were filled.

She spoke to one of her sons, "Bring me another jar."

"There aren't any more left." And at that precise moment, the oil stopped flowing.

When the widow reported the good news to Elisha, he said, "Go and sell the oil. Pay what you owe. You and your sons can live on what is left."

Incredible! Just as the widow thought all was lost, she experienced grace. God's love for His people extends to all need.

Today's Elishas at Work

In the New Testament Jesus established more humane ways of dealing with the poor, especially women and children. His compassion for the father-less and widows and the practices of the early church to provide for their needs established a pattern or model for Christian charity.

Nevertheless, poverty and its resulting human needs have not been eradicated in our own time. Just as in Old Testament times, poverty leaves the poor vulnerable to exploitation and oppression by those more wealthy or powerful. According to the 1999 guidelines from the US Department of Health and Human Services, a person earning less than $8,240 a year is poor. Most Americans are unaware that 1 percent of families in wealth own about as much as 95 percent of the rest of the population.

For a family of eight, the poverty level is considered $27,980 a year. As groups, Blacks, individuals in female-headed households, and Hispanics have poverty rates exceeding the country's average.

What does this actually mean for women and children? According to *Another Perspective* by John Cannon the following facts are true:[1]

1. The number of children living in extreme poverty has doubled since 1970.
2. One-quarter of children officially designated poor live in a family with at least one parent working full time year-round. These people are commonly known as the working poor.
3. Even if all poor single mothers obtained full-time jobs at their potential wage rates, a full 35 percent would still not be earning enough to escape poverty.
4. Two-thirds of minimum wage earners are female.
5. A person working full-time at minimum wage receives earnings that place him or her below the acknowledged poverty line for a family of two.

Certain societal factors further endanger the security of women in wage-earning capacities. The increase of out-of-wedlock births, especially among teenagers, has a huge detrimental effect. Girls under 17 who give birth are more likely to be poor; stay longer in poverty; have fewer opportunities to develop job skills; have less education; and, as a result, receive lower salaries. Single mothers have great difficulty finding affordable childcare.

Generally, women are paid less than men performing the same job. Drugs and alcohol are easily available to those who have lost hope and live in desperation. Drug dependency, although not exclusively a gender problem, does entrap many women.

Just as the widow of 2 Kings appealed to Elisha, women in poverty today cry out for our help. Their situations have reached the level of desperation. Our questions echo those of Elisha: How can we help you? Tell us. What do you have?

The apparent answer, nothing, begs our help. Can we, like Elisha, help them determine what they possess, regardless of how well hidden and insufficient? What can they do? Where are the dreams so long hidden away? Who can assess the potential? What is lacking? What resources do they need? Can their empty "jars" be filled with hope and joyful anticipation of a new life of possibility?

Catherine (not her real name) had given up. She had arrived at a dead end. Fleeing an abusive relationship in Michigan, she found herself in a shelter for battered women in Tupelo, Mississippi. She arrived with no plans, no expectations. Little did she know that her life was about to change drastically.

Group Night was announced at the shelter, and all residents were expected to attend. As the guest speaker, Julie Busby, spoke, Catherine's heart began to beat faster.

"I'm here to tell you about a program available to anyone here. It is called Christian Women's Job Corps, and the next session begins in July." As Julie continued to describe the job training program, Catherine became more and more interested. When Julie asked for a response, Catherine indicated her desire to join the program. Only one problem stood in her way. She was pregnant. Her baby was due the first week in August, right in the middle of the eight-week Christian Women's Job Corps (CWJC) session.

Catherine had moved to Tupelo after having endured not only regular beatings by one man but also a rape by another man, which had resulted in her pregnancy. At 18 years of age, she already had a 3-year-old daughter. How she wanted a new start! It had been a long time since she had experienced the sense of hope that she did that night.

"Please, Julie. Could I start classes, take a week off when the baby comes, and enter classes again?" Being with the group would give Catherine the emotional support she needed during this trying time in her life.

Catherine began classes with the other new members, and group members immediately began to bond with one another. On the second day of class, after experiencing the presence of Christ in every component of the program, the money management teacher led Catherine in a prayer to accept Christ as her personal Savior.

On August 9, Catherine's baby was born. Before she met Christ, she had planned to give up the baby for adoption, but after praying much about it, she decided to keep her new son. Although she did not know how she would take care of him, she had perfect peace with her decision. When her classmates visited her in the hospital, collectively they named the new baby Ezekiel, which means "gift of God" or "messenger."

Catherine had been permitted to stay at the shelter before her baby came, but after leaving the hospital, she had to move to an apartment. When Julie inspected the apartment, she stood transfixed, appalled at what she saw. The place seemed to be in total disarray. All the donated items had been tossed randomly about the floor, and Catherine's personal items were stuffed into garbage bags. Julie reported the situation to the women in the class, and they immediately swung into action. Kim said she would take Catherine and her children into her home for the rest of the week. Meanwhile, the others agreed to straighten and clean the apartment.

On cleaning day, Greta was late to class. When questioned about this, she admitted that she had been at the local dollar store, praying herself down each aisle. In spite of having no money to spare, Greta had bought everything Catherine would need to set up housekeeping—sheets and blankets, mop, broom, cleaning supplies, and other necessities. She had even taken from her personal supply of "luxury" to give Catherine bath oil and lotion so she would feel special while taking care of her two children alone. Greta says she has never missed the money.

Marilyn provided a personal support to Catherine, telling her of the power of prayer, assuring her that God would provide for a decision that honors Him. Her tangible gift to Catherine was a kitchen table and chairs, the only items salvaged from a fire in her own home.

After missing only two weeks of classes, Catherine finished the CWJC program. Ask her what her dreams for the future are, and Catherine has a ready response. "I want to go to school and become a social worker or teacher, so I can give back some of what others have given me." In the meantime, she has a job, which enables her to care for her children. "Best of all, everyone who knows her has seen the tremendous spiritual transformation," says Julie. "She cannot get enough of the Scriptures, and is growing by leaps and bounds."

Just as Elisha sought resources that miraculously sustained the poor widow in his day, Julie and other Christians seek to discover present-day miracles. Through the powerful acts of God many have moved from poverty to economic self-sufficiency, from this world's hopelessness to eternal salvation, through the Elishas of every age.

In Sylna Rego we find another modern-day Elisha. A missionary with the North American Mission Board, Sylna directs ministries to meet a variety of human needs, including the Living Water Care Center and Free Clinic, the Seafarer's House, and the Jericho Youth mentoring program. No program existed, however, to meet the needs of a young woman referred to Sylna by a Christian psychiatrist, who said, "This young woman needs a healthy environment and on-the-job training to get her into the workforce and out of welfare."

What Sylna did have was an opening for a critically needed clerical volunteer. The young woman, called Sharon by Sylna, was hired on the spot.

Sylna guided Sharon as she began to master working techniques, such as being on time and organizing priorities. They had times together of prayer and Scripture reading, and Sylna encouraged Sharon, contributing to her self-esteem. Sylna acknowledges that "God did the rest." As a result, Sharon began to blossom into an intelligent and eager-to-learn young woman. With the help of her counselor, Sharon's family was getting back on track.

Five months later Sharon surprised Sylna, as she sat in her office. Tears ran down her cheeks as she thanked Sylna for being her mentor. Her plans now were to go back to school for a master's degree in social work.

"None of you here at Gulf Stream Association will ever know how much you changed my life. I was ready to give up and you gave me your hand and showed me God was also holding my hand. I will be forever grateful."

An awareness of the needs of women may result in the question, What must be done? A more practical question might be, What should I do about it? Statistics alone cannot give the answer. Consider this story.

Mark Weible served as pastor of a small church in San Antonio before becoming a church starter strategist in multicultural communities in Galveston, Texas, for the North American Mission Board. Although the church's membership was small and not wealthy, their WMU director had a large missions heart and led the church to considerable involvement in their community and around the world. "Delpha Brown always had us exposed to the needs and busy helping to meet those needs. However, I was afraid she had gone too far one Sunday morning," Reverend Weible recalled.

Delpha had declared the day Undies Sunday. She reminded church members that homeless people sometimes receive good used clothing, but seldom ever do they receive new underwear. Therefore, she encouraged church members to buy packages of underwear for men, women, boys, and girls. When they arrived at the church building, they saw a clothesline draped with underwear of all sizes and shapes and stretched across the choir loft—Delpha's reminder of the day's assignment.

Mark looked out anxiously over his little flock. "The folks are really not going to like this!" he thought. "They won't consider having a clothesline full of underwear conducive to a worshipful atmosphere."

Just then his heart returned to the baptismal service he was about to begin, and his eyes fell on the first candidate, Starr.

Starr, living in a homeless shelter at the time, attended Christian Women's Job Corps® (CWJC℠) training. She had become a Christian as a result of the living testimony of some of the women of the church who had befriended her through CWJC. They invited her into their homes for dinner, provided transportation for her, and looked after her other needs.

As Mark stood in the baptistry that morning, about to open the worship service with a clothesline of underwear draped across the choir loft and serving as the picture frame of the baptism that was about to take place, he prayed for wisdom. Instantly, God gave the answer. A year earlier, as a part of a WMU emphasis, Delpha had challenged the church to begin thinking of the ways their little church could help the homeless. Now those months later they were about to baptize someone who was homeless on the day set aside as an ingathering of underwear for the homeless.

As Mark was about to place Starr under the baptismal waters, it all came to him. "Folks, this is what Christianity's all about," gesturing to the clothesline, "finding a need, meeting it, and loving the individual into God's kingdom."

The worshipers left church that morning with tears in their eyes, commenting to their pastor, "This was the best service our church ever had." Later that day Starr received her CWJC diploma and the members of Kingsborough Ridge Baptist Church came to cheer her on. Starr has since been employed, and she and her husband have rented an apartment across the street from the church where she helped in the church's multihousing ministry to the community. She is now a trainer for CWJC in San Antonio.

YOU? AN ELISHA?

Hopefully, reading this chapter has caused you to ask yourself certain questions. What do you have that you can use to assist the poor in your community? What is needed? What can you do?

Many community organizations provide food and clothing, but few offer resources in job assistance. Welfare reform programs have forced many women off welfare assistance without sufficient training to hold jobs that yield adequate wages. They have merely changed categories from the Unemployed to the Working Poor. Can you help?

Christian Women's Job Corps has met the needs of thousands of women in recent years. A volunteer-led ministry, CWJC moves women from welfare to economic independence, in a Christian context. Training for local site coordinators is held in various locations throughout the year. In addition to these coordinators, women serve as mentors and teachers of job and life skills and the Bible. Volunteers also assist in childcare, transportation, and meals for the classes. If your community already has a CWJC, visit the site for yourself to discover how you can be involved. If there is no local CWJC, pray that someone will feel led to begin one. Maybe you, Elisha?[2]

Assisting women—or men and children—only to improve their financial circumstances is a noble cause. Leading them to the abundant life in Christ is a heavenly cause. Elisha gave us a good example. Give a hand up, not a handout, to those who want more out of life than just a job. When you do, you will see miracles take place.

---

[1]*Another Perspective* (www.concentric.net/~jcannon/advoc128.html).
[2]For more information about Christian Women's Job Corps, contact your state WMU office or the national WMU office, or visit the WMU Web site at www.wmu.com.

3

Touched by an Angel

Current television and book themes reflect the growing national interest in angels. One of the most popular current TV programs, *Touched by an Angel*, centers around two angels, a beautiful Irish lass named Monica and her older supervisor, Tess. While the story line may not always coincide with the view of angels you have formed through Bible study, millions of viewers experience stories of forgiveness and restoration each week through these programs.

The presence of angels also makes hot items of jewelry, greeting cards, and knickknacks. But as Billy Graham discovered in research for a book about angels, little has been written about angels in this century. Although we have stereotypical visual images of angels, most people know little about what the Bible actually has to say about them. Normally, they are depicted as beautiful, winged female creatures with a harp in folded hands. The term *angelic* has come to imply gentleness, joy, and peace. But one author projects a different idea:

"They're not cute, cuddly, comfortable, chummy, or 'cool'. They are fearsome and formidable. They are huge. They are warriors."[1]

This description is quite consistent with scriptural accounts, where angels are usually depicted as male and often the bearers of warnings or threats. Always they are messengers of God. An account of the appearance of angels is recorded in 2 Kings 6:8–23. In this passage, they appear as soldiers in the eyes of Elisha's servant.

ANGELS IN SOLDIER'S ATTIRE

The king of Syria called a conference with his commanders. For some time his army had been warring with Israel. "Here," said the king, his index finger marking the precise place on the map before him, "Here is the place we will make camp." *(Paraphrase.)*

Some distance away but almost simultaneously, Elisha called his servant to him. "Quickly, go to our king, the king of Israel. Tell him that under no circumstance should he pass this place, for the king of Syria and his armies will be there." And Elisha gave him the name of the Syrian's encampment. Several times this scenario repeated itself. The king of Israel was saved, along with his army, by having advance notice of the location of the Syrians.

The king of Syria raged. How could Israel's king constantly escape? Finally, he became convinced: a traitor must lie within his own ranks. He called a meeting of his staff to discover the guilty one. "Who of us works on behalf of the king of Israel?" he demanded.

"None, my lord, O king," answered one of his men with frustration. "But Elisha, the prophet who is in Israel, tells the king of Israel the words you speak, even in the privacy of your bedroom."

"Go then," ordered the king, "and find out where this Elisha is so that we might capture him."

When his men discovered Elisha in the city of Dothan, the king ordered that a great army, outfitted with horses and chariots, be deployed to capture him. They arrived at their destination at night and completely surrounded the city. Early the next morning, Elisha's servant arose, dressed, and went outside to begin preparations for the day. What he saw brought terror to his heart. The Syrian army, with its horses and chariots, surrounded the city. "Alas, my master, what shall we do?"

Elisha, with a quiet assurance that comes only from God, answered, "Fear not, for those who are with us are more than those who are with them." Then, in order to give proof to the young man, Elisha prayed, "O Lord, I pray Thee, open his eyes that he may see."

With this, the servant's eyes were opened wide, allowing him to see the mountain full of horses and chariots of fire around Elisha, God's mighty defense. As the Syrian army came down to capture Elisha, he prayed once again, "Strike this people, I pray thee, with blindness." Immediately, the Syrian soldiers became blind.

Elisha faced the army and said, "You have come to the wrong city. I know this man, Elisha, you are looking for. Follow me, and I'll take you right to him."

Elisha led them to Samaria, the capital city of Israel. Once again he prayed, and the eyes of the Syrian army were opened. Imagine their surprise when the first thing they saw was the king of Israel!

"What shall we do, Elisha? Kill them?" asked the king.

"No, my lord. Set bread and water before them, so that they may eat and return to their master," advised the prophet. After a great feast, the Syrians were sent away, never to attack Israel again.

"Greater are those who are with us than those who are with them." Elisha had reference to the reality of

unseen but actual spiritual forces available not only
to prophets but equally to every person of faith. The
fearful servant needed to see the reinforcements to
believe they were there.

Does God allow certain people today to see other-
wise invisible objects, angels, for example, to under-
gird their faith? When you hear reports of the
sighting of angels, do you merely roll your eyes and
think no one could be so naïve as to believe those
reports? Or do you react with wonderment, not quite
sure what you believe? Are you confident that God
does indeed perform miracles, even in spontaneous
healings, or do you pass it off with a shrug of your
shoulders? Many can recount events that are truly
"beyond belief."

ANGELS ON THE ROOF

In 1965 the Communist Party of Indonesia was surprisingly the third largest in the world, surprisingly
because the large majority of the Indonesian populace embraced Islam. How could one who also
declared, "There is one God, and His name is Allah"
embrace a philosophy that included atheism?

Communist leaders cunningly dealt with the
matter of religion. "Oh," they seemed to say, "No
problem. Indonesian Communism is different. It
allows religion to coexist with Communism. In fact,
we have a slogan that lifts up that tenet—
NASACOM." This acronym brought together three
ideals: nationalism, religion *(agama)*, and Communism. In order to popularize this strange union, officials declared NASACOM as the official slogan for the
Independence Day celebration on August 17.

Indonesians celebrated Independence Day over
several days and always with parades and hand-
crafted decorations. The Communist hammer and

sickle was prominently displayed throughout the towns and villages. Huge billboards, as well as graffiti on the walls, praised the virtues of Communism and reviled the evils of America. It was evident that nationalism and Communism had been merged, but what about religion? Muslims and Christians alike, while harboring great resentment toward the deceptive slogan, quietly endured, for the time being, the parading of NASACOM before the people.

Southern Baptists missionaries had entered Indonesia in 1951. While the work went unhampered in the early years, serious resistance had recently emerged. Missionaries were accused of being spies for the CIA. Every attempt was made to stir up suspicion of the churches. The Baptist hospital in the small town of Kediri was known far and wide for its superb medical care, but even it was the focus of some foment.

Dr. Kathleen Jones was informed of the unrest in the Kediri hospital when she came from the other Baptist hospital in Sumatra to relieve Dr. Win Applewhite who was going on stateside assignment. Later discoveries pointed to a Communist labor union as the source of trouble. "Soon these missionaries will have to leave," the union leaders reported to the hospital employees, "and then your Communist brothers will take over. We promise you better jobs and higher salaries." They sought every opportunity to strengthen the suspicion directed toward the foreign (international) missionaries.

Communist labor union leaders found the perfect opportunity on Saturday, August 14. The hospital chaplain had announced in a staff meeting that, like it or not, NASACOM was the designated slogan as decreed by the government and had to be used in the decorations. Unfortunately, one missionary doctor was not aware of this requirement, and he was incensed upon seeing the slogan in front of the hospital. He took it down and went to the hospital office for clarification. While the sign was down for no more than 30 minutes, an employee falsely reported to the authorities that the doctor had taken down the sign, stepped on it, and criticized national president Sukarno.

Within minutes representatives from the police, military, and other government offices gathered at the hospital, demanding an explanation. In addition, the chaplain found a revolt among the employees brewing because of the reported actions. While the chaplain was able to calm down the employees, public outrage only grew.

The following Saturday, August 21, a representative from the police department informed Jones that on Monday a delegation would be calling on the hospital. It was further announced that this meant a demonstration, and she should be prepared for trouble. Another missionary left immediately to confer with the American consulate in Surabaja, a one-and-a-half-hour drive away, where American officials underscored the serious nature of the situation and once again advised preparation.

How do you prepare for such impending disaster? Other demonstrations toward American entities, including the American embassy, had resulted in destruction. For the entire week Jones attempted to improve relations, with little or no results. The offending doctor, along with his family, was ordered to leave the country immediately.

Jones found that she had friends in the midst of the chaos. People from all walks of life came to her, indicating their support. Missionaries and pastors in other areas were praying about the demonstration to be held on Monday, August 23. Others around the world were praying, too, without any awareness of the great need, but because it was Win Applewhite's birthday.

On Sunday night Jones claimed Psalm 91 (NRSV), reading the promises time after time: "He will deliver you from the snare of the fowler; . . . He will cover you with his pinions, and under His wings you will find refuge. . . . You will not fear the terror of the night, or the . . . destruction that wastes at noonday. . . . Because you have made the Lord your refuge, . . . no evil shall befall you, no scourge come near your tent. For he will command his angels concerning you to guard you in all your ways. On their hands they will bear you up, so that you will not dash your foot against a stone."

Monday morning. The day had arrived. Jones and the chaplain walked through each section of the hospital, giving encouragement to the patients and the employees and asking them to read Psalm 91. Although they had been told to keep the entrance hall empty to avoid injury in the event of forced entry, patients and employees intent on standing by Jones filled the space.

Meanwhile, several thousand demonstrators gathered at a soccer field to hear anti-American speeches. Sufficiently aroused, the crowd began its march toward the hospital, shouting, "Down with America," and carrying paint, rocks, and containers of kerosene.

Kathleen Jones was scheduled to meet a committee of 20 in the chapel. Although the faces of a number of persons in the group were very familiar to her, these individuals refused to look at her as they entered the room. In the formal portion of the meeting a letter was read identifying the American missionaries as spies and making certain demands. Jones quietly and calmly thanked them for their suggestions, and the group left.

Now came the time for the crowd to begin the destructive acts. Never before had a demonstration proceeded to this point without damage, destruction, or deaths. When the committee emerged from the hospital, the crowd yelled, shouting familiar Communist slogans and hatred toward the American spies.

Looking to their leaders for a signal for attack, the mob was surprised to see the committee continue out the door and down the street, headed for the mayor's office. Confused, they fell into step and arrived at city hall for the presentation of their letter to the mayor. By then, hot heads had cooled and no one seemed to have the taste for rioting.

A miracle! No one was hurt; the hospital was untouched. A great expression of thanksgiving was lifted for God's providential acts! On that day many people marveled at God's mercy and grace.

What had prompted the demonstrators to leave without completing their purposes? Why, while holding the elements of destruction in their hands, did they simply turn and walk away?

Later reports indicated that some of the Indonesians had witnessed an incredible scene. On the roof of the hospital several angels stood watch over the demonstration. No missionaries saw them. Perhaps they were not really there. Could it be, however, that those who needed assurance that they should not be afraid, for "there are more with us than there are with them," were given an angelic visitation just as Elisha's servant so long ago? (2 Kings 6:16, *paraphrase*)

Jones, the chaplain, and others who went to the various areas of the hospital afterwards found the hospital employees stunned. They could not believe the building had been untouched. God had preserved the hospital building and its staff. It was truly a miracle!

If you pray for missionaries on their birthdays, you had a part in this "beyond belief" event. Furthermore, Jones reports that during the seven months of the attempted Communist coup beginning on Independence Day, a number of crises could have affected missions work in Indonesia. Each of these crises occurred on the birthday of a missionary to Indonesia. Just by chance? A coincidence?

Because of the paucity of books on angelology, Billy Graham set out to write a book entitled *Angels, God's Secret Agents*. In explaining why he wrote this book, Graham said: "I am convinced that these heavenly beings exist and that they provide unseen aid on our behalf. . . . I believe in angels because the Bible says there are angels; and I believe the Bible to be the true Word of God. I also believe in angels because I have sensed their presence in my life on special occasions."[2]

Ask other devout Christians about their belief in angels, and do not be surprised when they relate a personal experience in which angels were involved.

ANGELS UNDERGROUND

At 3:02 A.M., Tuesday, August 17, 1999, an earthquake registering 7.4 on the Richter scale, with the most powerful tremor ever recorded in the region, threw sleeping residents of the country of Turkey from their beds and sent them into the streets in panic. While the earthquake's epicenter was near the city of Izmet, dozens of buildings collapsed in Istanbul, 65 miles away. Ankara, 270 miles to the west, lost electrical power.

Rescue attempts began immediately; residents of Izmet dug in the rubble with their bare hands. Police joined in the search, but they lacked the heavy equipment necessary to raise entire walls that had collapsed on victims. In the hospitals injured people lay on the bare floors, as hospital workers were unable to cope with the flood of injured. Hundreds of dead bodies were wrapped in blankets, waiting for later collection.

By afternoon the local television stations reported that the death toll exceeded 1,000, with 10,000 injured. Those who witnessed the carnage knew the count would rise. Three days later the number of deaths climbed to more than 10,000, with 20,000 missing amid the collapsed buildings. Again it was announced that the number of deaths would certainly rise. Disaster relief volunteers began to pour into the area.

These rescuers worked tirelessly and heroically under insurmountable odds, but by Friday they began to lose hope. Seventy-two hours had passed, and it seemed impossible that anyone could live without food or water beyond this time. But amid the scenes of horror and death, a few incredible stories of survival arose.

On Sunday, August 22, 130 hours after the earthquake hit, rescuers pulled a paraplegic woman from under a collapsed building in the city of Golcuk. Later that day workers pulled another woman from the rubble of her apartment in Cinarcik, alive after 138 hours!

While rescue teams were departing from Turkey on Monday, August 23, a 4-year-old boy became the last to be saved from the devastation. For 140 hours, he had remained conscious but trapped in the layers of rubble. The boy's uncle, looking for dead bodies, shined a flashlight into a gap and saw his nephew's frightened face. Within minutes other rescuers joined forces to free the child. His mother had been rescued and was recuperating in the hospital, but his father and three sisters had not survived.

"Finding the boy was a miracle of God," said the uncle. The rest of the family had given up hope and had already prepared the child's grave. Incredible!

Perhaps the most awesome story failed to make the reports of BBC or even CNN. Maybe because it seemed beyond belief? In the city of Golcuk a French rescue team found two sisters, both still alive seven days after the earthquake. Missionary David Weston, living in Georgia on stateside assignment, had joined a disaster response from Woodstock Baptist Church. David talked to the men who had found and saved the girls and heard the details of the rescue. After they were extracted from the rubble, the girls began to inquire about two men.

The rescuers responded that they found no men. "Oh, you have to keep looking," the girls pleaded. "Two white-haired men brought us water every day. You have to find them." The rescue team went back to the site, but found no white-haired men.

Were they just figments of the girls' imaginations? Were the girls only seeing things as a result of bodily trauma? After all, they were buried for seven days. Then why were their bodies not dehydrated?

Was it possible that God had a reason for sending His emissaries to keep the girls alive? No Christian was there to share Christ. We have no assurance either girl will ever know of Christ's offer of salvation.

TOUCHED BY AN ANGEL

In Turkey today there are two girls to whom God sent messengers to perform a miracle. You know that someone has to tell them of Jesus. What can you do? Pray? Send missionaries? Become a missionary?

You cannot do nothing. You have been drawn into the spiritual fate of these girls. To one day be permitted to hear, "I was one of the girls saved miraculously, and now I know why. I want to trust Christ as my Savior," would be truly awesome—beyond belief.

Have you ever seen an angel? Probably not, since few people have; but many theologians think the appearance of angels has increased recently. In Bible accounts, angels often appeared just before world-changing or life-changing events. Whenever has humankind had a greater need for comfort than in this increasingly violent, scary world?[3]

What a comfort to know that God has commanded "his angels concerning you to guard you in all your ways. On their hands they will bear you up, so that you will not dash your foot against a stone" (Psalm 91:11,12 NRSV). He is an awesome God!

[1]Peter Kreeft, *Angels and Demons: What Do We Really Know About Them?* (San Francisco: Ignatius Press, 1995), 17.
[2]Billy Graham, *Angels: God's Secret Agents,* rev. and exp. (Minneapolis: Grason, 1986), 23–24.
[3]Kreeft, *Angels and Demons,* 18.

4

Going Too Far?

Alice Newman, executive director for WMU in Hawaii, holds the distinction of being the world's best hostess. If you are lucky enough to be her guest, she will greet you at the airport with lei and warm embrace. No one can make you feel more warmly welcomed. Each day you find a gift, a different specialty from her state, on the bedside table. You may see chocolate-covered macadamia nuts, Kona coffee, or some other Hawaiian treat. Her meals qualify for inclusion in any gourmet cookbook. At Christmastime, she bakes and cooks for days in preparation for a reception she hosts for a large group of co-workers, church members, and friends. All this, and Alice also wears more hats and works more hours in her job than anyone I know. She truly goes beyond all expectations in making her friends feel loved and appreciated.

You may know others who go out of their way for a designated purpose, but few compare with four men who lived in the days Jesus was beginning His ministry. Mark 2 records their story.

LOVE BEYOND BELIEF
The room was packed, with no space for even one more person to stand inside. People even crowded

the doors and windows. No radio or television broadcast was necessary to tell the people of Capernaum that Jesus had returned home; the grapevine had effectively alerted everyone of Jesus' itinerary.

Many in the crowd had heard Jesus the first time He taught in their synagogue, and they were astonished at the depth of his spirit. No scribe had ever before taught with such authority. Who could ever forget the confrontation between Jesus and the man with an unclean spirit right there in the synagogue!

"'What have you to do with us, Jesus of Nazareth? Have you come to destroy us? I know who you are, the Holy One of God'" (Mark 1:24 NRSV).

But Jesus countered with, "Be silent, and come out of him!" With that the unclean spirit came out of the poor man, convulsing him and crying in strange shrieks.

The crowd was amazed. "What is this? A new teaching! With authority he commands even the unclean spirits, and they obey him."

Later that day Jesus healed Simon Peter's mother-in-law, and with that began the endless stream of many in Capernaum who came for healing and deliverance from unclean spirits. Early the next morning Jesus prayed and determined to leave for other parts of Galilee, and from that day His fame spread everywhere throughout all Galilee.

Now Jesus had returned from His campaign throughout the region. Those who had heard Him the first time hungered to hear more of His teaching. The people who had not heard Him but heard reports of His teaching were intrigued and eager to make their own assessment of this articulate man of God. They pushed and shoved to get a place where they could hear every word.

Meanwhile, five men anxiously studied their dilemma. For some time they had awaited the return of Jesus. The paralytic man, the focus of their concern, had heard reports of miraculous healings. Was it possible that Jesus might heal him too?

He likely well remembered the onset of his paralysis. Imagine him awakening early one morning to numbness and the inability to control his arms and legs. In the next few hours he probably experienced great fear as the condition gradually drained away any ability to use his body. No doctor to make a diagnosis, no hospital to give treatment. Only the gradual awareness that this was for real. He was now a paralytic!

Not only was he unable to provide for his family, but also he now needed constant care himself. He had no workman's compensation, no health insurance. He would be a burden to his family for the rest of his life.

Perhaps his greatest concern, however, was what others would think. The belief passed down through the generations was that a person's sin brought certain punishment. What had he done that was so deadly serious as to bring consequences this devastating?

To his surprise, friends stood in the gap, offering countless remedies and many prayers. They promised to do anything to bring healing. And then Jesus came.

The four friends prepared the cot, placed their paralytic friend on it, and set out for the place where Jesus was staying. As they neared the home, they saw the huge crowd already gathered in and around the house. What could they do? It was clear they would never be able to work their way through this mass of people.

Suddenly, one man hit upon an idea, highly unusual but possible. If they could not make entrance through the door, they would do so through the roof!

Houses of that day commonly had an external stairway leading to the flat roof. Poles across the space between the walls framed the roof, with sticks and reeds interspersed. Matting and dirt hardened by the sun covered this frame, so it was easy to remove a segment of the roof, and just as easy to repair it.

Imagine the expressions of amazement as the crowd first felt debris raining down, and then, looking up, saw a man on a pallet slowly being lowered to the place where Jesus stood. How would Jesus respond to this surprising interruption?

Jesus saw the faith of the five men and said to the paralytic, "Son, your sins are forgiven."

The Hebrews believed that one needed to seek forgiveness before he could expect to be healed. Because of this, the afflicted man rejoiced at his forgiveness.

Others in the crowd were furious. The rabbis believed in a merciful, forgiving God, but Who was this upstart assuming the power of God, claiming the ability to forgive sins? A blasphemer, no doubt. Who did He think He was?

Jesus, knowing of their criticism, responded to them directly, "'Why do you raise such questions in your hearts? Which is easier, to say to the paralytic "Your sins are forgiven," or to say, "Stand up and take your mat and walk"? But so that you may know that the Son of Man has authority on earth to forgive sins'—he said to the paralytic— 'I say to you, stand up, take your mat and go to your home'" (Mark 2:8–10 NRSV).

As long as the healed man lived, he remembered the day he became whole—spiritually and physically. He worshiped God Who is all-powerful, Who performs miracles of forgiveness and healing. But there was more. He remembered his four friends. Without their willingness to go beyond the expected, he might never have met Christ face-to-face. Without their faith, he would still be helplessly lying on his pallet of infirmity. The miracle of God was made possible by the faith of mortals.

BEYOND THE EXPECTED IN BOSNIA

This gospel story testifies to God's power and grace, but also acknowledges a "beyond belief" act of loving friends. While it would be much more difficult to replay this ancient story exactly today, occasionally friends, and even strangers, go beyond the expected to help others. We sometimes read those stories in newspapers, but most often we are unaware of those heroic acts. It is unfortunate, for these stories of exceptional concern and courage are often beyond belief.

Between 1998 and 2000, Woman's Missionary Union focused its attention on Project HELP℠: Violence. It proved to be a very timely emphasis, for war, destruction, and crime had reached epidemic proportions at home and around the world. In an effort to find a suitable international ministry project, WMU staff conducted a survey to identify a country suffering postwar devastation. One area stood out above all others in violence and need: the former Yugoslavia.

Since the time of Christ, the area of Yugoslavia has been the seat of unrest. Even in the early days of turmoil, ethnic diversity lay at the core of the hostilities. Historically, Roman Catholic Croats, Orthodox

Serbs, and Muslims have called this area home. In May 1993, a conflict between Croats and Muslims, associated with brutal ethnic cleansing, resulted in thousands of casualties. In March 1994, however, when Serbian forces attacked Bosnian Muslims and Croats, the latter two groups ended hostilities and formed a joint federation to fight the Orthodox Serbs. NATO forces entered the battle, and by late summer 1995 the Muslim-Croat federation controlled more than 50 percent of the country's territory. Lengthy negotiations between the US assistant secretary of state and the presidents of Bosnia, Croatia, and Serbia resulted in the Dayton Peace Accord. Designed to guarantee a lasting peace in Bosnia, it formed a single state made up of two entities, the Federation of Bosnia and Herzegovina, and the Serb Republic.

Between 100,000 and 250,000 people were killed in the war, mostly Muslims. Some 2.3 million people were displaced from their homes within and outside the country. The International Criminal Tribunal for the Former Yugoslavia indicted for atrocities more than 50 Bosnians, mostly Serbs. The ensuing years have been characterized by turbulence, brutality, and death.

If WMU members were looking for a war-torn country with devastation and an uneasy political situation, they needed not look any further. Predominantly Muslims, the Bosnians were living in bombed-out homes, and sharing their land with the multitudes swarming in from Kosovo. Nowhere could these women find greater need.

Their first two scheduled projects to Bosnia had to be cancelled because the situation grew too dangerous for foreigners to enter. In the summer of 1999, however, a team of 12 medical volunteers arrived in Sarajevo. Eight nurses, 1 dental hygienist, and 3 doctors in training made up the team. Wanda Lee, then national WMU president (now WMU executive director) and a nurse herself, said, "Our purpose in going was to meet human needs in such a way that God would be seen and the doors would be opened for others to share Christ in the days to come."

Members of Baptist Nursing Fellowship had collected a mountain of medicines, supplies, and equipment for the team to use. The first hang-up came when customs officials confiscated the medicines. Like the four friends in Mark 2 who were not defeated by what seemed an impossible situation, the nurses still began to plan for their medical ministry in Bosnia. The medicines were released five days after they were confiscated.

After a brief survey of needs and resources, team members realized their work would be difficult. First they would need to set up clinics in strategic areas. The large number of Kosovar refugees had been located in tent encampments throughout the area and had great medical needs.

Teams formed, composed of one journeyman or International Service Corps (ISC) missionary, one national translator, and two volunteers. Although the missionaries were relatively new to Bosnia and were actually on two-year assignments, they did yeoman's service in leading these teams of volunteers.

Two especially critical cases surfaced during the very first day of clinic. The first, a refugee from Kosovo, had received a kidney from his father ten years earlier. Because he had fled Kosovo so quickly, he had no medicine and very little money. One particular medication, Imuran, was absolutely necessary to help this transplant patient avoid rejection of the

kidney. Where could he find such an unusual medication, and how could he ever pay for it?

Initially the man had been placed in a tent city,
but as the rains came and the refugees needed better
quarters, relief workers relocated him to a school for
the blind, which had been temporarily closed. The
nurses had set up one of their clinics in a room at
the school.

Wanda tried to assure the man that they would
find his medicine, as difficult as that might prove to
be. Bosnian citizens can get prescriptions from their
doctor and usually get the medicine free. But for this
man, a Kosovar, and a refugee at that, chances of his
securing the medicine were slim to none.

Wanda also met a woman at that first clinic. She
brought her baby with her, but her six-year-old son
who had cerebral palsy lay in the local hospital. She,
too, had only a little money and a limited supply of
her son's medicine. Finding his medicine seemed an
impossible job, for it was German-made and not
approved in Bosnia.

Two gigantic tasks the very first day! With all the
other needs, would it not be better to give up before
even beginning to look? Why spend time on a hopeless search? You could no more have dissuaded
Wanda from looking for the needed medications
than you could the paralyzed man's friends from dismantling that roof.

Wanda learned that there were pharmacies that
would sell medications if you knew the name and
dosage and had enough money to buy them—without a prescription. She had her plan of action. She
saw both the man and the mother several times that
week. Each time, the young woman showed Wanda
the dwindling supply of her son's medication. The
man was apparently in satisfactory condition and

always expressed his gratitude to Wanda for trying to find his medicine.

Wanda went from pharmacy to pharmacy without luck for a week, but with the help of a Bosnian attorney—and God—she did the impossible. She found the man's medicine! She could not wait to take it to the school to give it to him.

When Wanda arrived at the school, however, the man had been moved to another tent city, and no one knew where he was. For days when she was not working in a clinic, she went with the interpreter and a missionary to look for the man. On the last day she was in Bosnia, she went to the last tent city with a heavy heart. If they did not find him there, the chances were great that he would not survive.

As the small group discussed their business with the officials in the office, a woman outside overheard their conversation.

"I think I can help you," she said. "The man you are seeking is my husband."

What rejoicing there was! Wanda had not seen the man's wife before, and had she not been nearby, perhaps the visit would have been fruitless.

What about the medication for the little boy? Is there also a "beyond belief" story about it? You may think it is even more incredible.

Wanda had attempted to find the unapproved medication in ten different pharmacies, all to no avail. Again, on the last day, Wanda went to the only pharmacy she had not visited. When her interpreter asked for the medicine, fully expecting a negative response, Wanda could not believe it when the pharmacist said she had it. With pounding heart, Wanda asked, "How much?"

When the pharmacist answered, "One hundred seventy-five dollars for a three-month supply,"

Wanda told her she wanted it, even though the price was great. She also told her she did not have the cash with her, but she would go get it and return later. "Ask her if she will please hold it for me until I return," she requested of her interpreter.

Instead of repeating the question to the pharmacist, the interpreter looked deeply into Wanda's eyes. Several times he had asked questions of the nurses' team, trying to understand why they had come, why they were willing to go out of their way for people they did not even know.

"You really do want this medicine, don't you?" he asked. Wanda assured him that she did.

"All right," he said, pulling money from his pocket. "I was just paid today. Please take my money for the medicine." The money represented his entire month's salary. Could he trust that she would repay the loan? Had this young man sensed a bit of God's love and desire not only to provide medicine for a little child but also a new understanding of the joy of ministering in His name? Wanda later repaid the young man, just as God so often gives back to us in abundance what we give to Him.

As a sidebar to the story, this young man, as well as another translator, made decisions to become Christians, and after the team had returned to the US, they were baptized.

Now to find the young mother. Their search was thwarted by the discovery that the child had been released from the hospital and the family had been relocated. They were just about to give up when the missionary and interpreter spotted a woman who looked like the young mother coming out of a grocery store. When they approached her, the mother saw the medicine and began to cry. Never had she believed they could find the medicine, much less be able to pay for it. The people who stood around might not have been sure why these, a Bosnian Muslim, a Kosovar Orthodox, an American missionary, and a visiting nurse were standing outside a grocery store, laughing, crying, and embracing. God, looking down on the scene, perhaps thought of the paralytic and the joy his friends experienced when he was healed. Just as Jesus had said on that occasion, "Your sins are forgiven," the missionary now had a foundation on which to take the same message to this Kosovar woman.

There is a postscript to this story. Reflecting on these experiences, Wanda says, "One last observation has served as a warning to me personally. Having seen the results of hatred, racial and religious intolerance, each of us must be more active in doing what we can to eliminate this from our society or we could very well be the next Bosnia or Kosovo or Sudan. Our emphasis on Project HELP: Violence could not have come at a more crucial time. God is always ahead of us, isn't He?"

LAYING DOWN ONE'S LIFE

John 15:13 (NRSV) reveals the ultimate test of love: "No one has greater love than this, to lay down one's life for one's friends."

People across America saw this depth of love played out June 1, 1999, after American Airlines Flight 1420, in the midst of a thunderstorm, crashed on its way to Little Rock, Arkansas. On board were 25 members of the Ouachita Singers tour group from Ouachita Baptist University.

The students; their director, Charles Fuller; and others making the trip had anticipated it for several months. The original itinerary would have taken them to China, but largely because of the tenuous nature of national relationships, their destination was changed to Germany. Camille Simmons, associational missionary in the San Antonio Baptist Association of Texas, and mother of choir members Mark and Jim, was happier with the change, but still felt a disquieting within. With a strong faith and belief in the power of prayer, Camille knew what it was to trust God, but she was led to pray for God to spare her boys' lives.

The students' experiences on the tour had been life-changing through the concerts in schools, on the streets, and in churches of the former East Germany where few missionaries serve. Singing for and visiting with Kosovar refugees in Austria gave special significance to being in that place at that time. Their three-week stay left them with treasured memories. As the last days of their trip approached, the students' thoughts turned toward home. They were almost home when the unthinkable happened.

Jeffrey Root, assistant to the president for public relations for Ouachita Baptist University, in "The Southern Baptist Educator" (vol. 64, no. 1) wrote: "In the minutes after Flight 1420 crashed, the 25 members of the Singers' tour group were, as one passenger put it, 'a choir of angels.' Some of the Singers literally carried injured passengers across waist- and chest-high water, while others pulled people from the plane."

Mark and Jim had been seated in the exit row and were thus responsible for opening the exit door. Neither the first pull nor the second could dislodge it. Finally, Mark jerked with all his strength and was rewarded by the release of the door, making clear this crucial exit. He stayed beside a man who had two broken legs until help arrived.

Misha Perkins jumped through the flames to exit the plane. Her slight frame and night blindness kept her from assisting people from the plane, but outside she found many needs. She moved toward the most critically wounded, Fred Agag, who had sustained a deep cut in his lower abdomen. Lying in the driving rain and hail, he was going into shock. Misha used her own body to warm and protect him, while calming him with her words of comfort. She sang "Amazing Grace" and recited Psalm 91. Because of her actions, Agag survived.

James Harrison, a Ouachita senior majoring in church music, assisted a number of passengers off the plane. After all had exited who were able, James continued to search for those who needed help. Because of the heavy smoke, he died in the aisle near the back of the plane. Did James hear Jesus' whisper, "No one has greater love than this, to lay down one's life for one's friends"? He had made the supreme sacrifice out of love.

LAYING DOWN OUR LIVES FOR ONE ANOTHER

John, the disciple of love, spoke often of love's demands. The verse from his gospel most often committed to memory, John 3:16, extols the degree of God's love that compelled him to give His one and only Son to secure our salvation. Only in heaven will we know the full significance of this sacrifice. Toward the end of John's life, he reiterated the dimensions of God's love in 1 John 3:16 (NRSV): "We know love by this, that he laid down his life for us."

But John does not end his message there. He continues with these words: "And we ought to lay down our lives for one another."

If you could only prove your love for God by giving your life, would you do it?

But wait! Finish John's thoughts from 1 John 3:17 (NRSV): "How does God's love abide in anyone who has the world's goods and sees a brother or sister in need and yet refuses help?"

Our love may never be tested by the requirement of dying for someone else, but we can be confident that we are tested daily by the demand to live for others. In this big world filled with need, our love must make a difference. We must pray each day that our love forces us to see the poor and dying, here at home and around the world. We hear the expression, "Out of sight, out of mind," and we have no intention to let sight invade our minds. We stick to safe, comfortable circles that shield us from the human need just beyond our view.

Would you be willing to go out of your way to seek those who are in need? Will you involve your life in theirs? Charter a bus for your church, and drive around to identify areas of poverty. Ask those serving areas of high crime how you might be helpful. "Oh, but those are dangerous areas. I might get hurt," you say. Ray Bakke, a noted urbanologist, has said, "There are some places in the city where only a woman can go." Because women are met with trust and lack of fear, we can be quite safe in most areas of the city. Do you dare go to the place of real need? Can you go beyond the ordinary, for the love of God?

5

Harvest in Albania

*G*ardening has always been a passion with me. In my high school years I watched my father tenderly coax growth out of the dry soil of west Texas. Gardenias and roses do not exactly thrive in that part of Texas, but Dad loved them and felt that the extra attention and work were worth it when a single bud burst forth.

While living in Richmond I experimented with a small postage stamp-sized garden. The woman next door was my inspiration. In the spring, when danger of freezing weather was over, she began to work in her garden, tilling the garden plot and adding fertilizer and lime to enrich the soil. During the middle of summer she had luscious tomatoes, green beans (they're called snaps there), squash, and other garden fruits. With her help and example, I, too, supplied our kitchen with wonderful vegetables for several years.

Squirrels, those cute furry things, were the bane of our existence. They watched the progress of the tomatoes as closely as I did, and at the first show of red ripeness, I could expect to see stolen bites from the choicest ones.

Women farmers like me had to fight the elements, and sometimes it appeared that drought or an overabundance of rain would steal the yield of my

garden. Aphids and other insects could strip a plant
before I knew it. Constant vigil is necessary in the
growth of tender plants.

God continues to plant His Church in our world
today. He, too, is embattled by elements bent on
destruction. While we humans are bound to time
and place, however, God sees the beginning from the
end. Temporary setbacks, while causing delay, cannot stay the final victory of the Church.

PLANTING THE SEED IN ALBANIA

Do you know someone who has made a dramatic
turnaround in his life? Who was once active in hate
crimes and is now campaigning for peace? Who
could have been described as a rabid legalist and now
seeks to understand law as only a guide to right living? Do you know someone who was once proud of
his heritage and background, but now describes himself as the worst of the worst? Has this person left his
life's goal to become somebody to being satisfied
wherever he is, in whatever circumstances? Has he
left a career of prominence to become an evangelist
to the world? If so, you may be thinking of Saul of
Tarsus, whose life sustained a remarkable change.

Many other followers of Christ were equally committed to be faithful to God's vision for His people
during the first century's evolution of the Church,
but they stayed in the land of their birth. They saw
the growth of the Church in Jerusalem, Antioch,
Damascus, and other areas of Palestine. What thrust
Paul out into a larger sphere to evangelize? Certainly,
Paul had traveled more extensively than the fisher-
men and tax collectors Jesus also touched, and that
possibly gave him a broader vision for the world. For
whatever reason, God used Paul dramatically in the
expansion of the gospel.

Look in the back of a Bible at the maps that show Paul's three missionary journeys and his trip to Rome. You can clearly see the thousands of miles he traveled, by foot, boat, donkey, or carriage. We have to read of his experiences in Acts or in his letters to churches to know the details of the successes and failures in his proclamation. He was shipwrecked, beaten, expelled from cities, and even jailed in his passion for the gospel.

Look again at the maps. Modern-day Greece, Crete, and the Balkans first heard the gospel during Paul's time. The trade routes from east to west made the western expansion possible, and the many Roman settlements further facilitated the move into Europe. In Romans 15:18–21 (CEV), Paul sums up his work: "All I will talk about is how Christ let me speak and work, so that the Gentiles would obey him. Indeed, I will tell how Christ worked miracles and wonders by the power of the Holy Spirit. I have preached the good news about him all the way from Jerusalem to Illyricum. But I have always tried to preach where people have never heard about Christ. I am like a builder who doesn't build on anyone else's foundation. It is just as the Scriptures say, 'All who haven't been told about him will see him, and those who haven't heard about him will under-stand.'"

In this passage Paul indicates that the furthest point of his evangelistic efforts was Illyricum. Look at your maps once more, and you will see that Illyricum is not on Paul's itinerary, but northwest of Philippi and Berea. Nowhere in Acts is this campaign noted. Did he possibly make an extension to that area while he was in Philippi? I would love to think that Lydia, Paul's first convert in Philippi, helped to subsidize that trip. She certainly had the financial means to do so. Did Paul discuss this area with her when he and his companions stayed in her home? If so, it would be most interesting when coupled with events in historical Illyricum in our own time.

During the time of Paul, Rome ruled Illyria. The Illyrians refused to be assimilated into the Roman culture, however, and their distinctive language and culture survived. Just as Paul stated, Christianity was fully preached in the area during the first century, and in A.D. 58 Paul placed an apostle in charge of the city of Epidamnus. By the fifth century Christianity had become the established religion, and from the eighth through the eleventh century, Illyria became known as Albania.

THE TENDER PLANT TESTED

Albanian cities expanded and commerce flourished as did the growth of art, culture, and education. However, the Ottomans (from present-day Turkey) invaded Albania in 1388, and in spite of their strong resistance, the Ottomans ruled Albania for four centuries. As Ottoman power declined in the eighteenth century, Albanian military lords rose up to dominate until 1822 when the Ottomans again overthrew them.

During the nineteenth century, a strong desire for independence united all Albanians, including those who made up the majority of the population in Kosovo. Between 1910 and 1912 Albanian nationalists rebelled against the Ottomans, and when the Western powers waged a simultaneous attack on the Ottomans, Albania immediately proclaimed its independence. Unfortunately, because of pressure from Albania's neighbors, the Western powers gave the Albanian-inhabited region of Kosovo to Serbia and much of the Cameria region to Greece, leaving half the Albanian population outside the country's borders. In 1920, Albania was admitted to the League of Nations, achieving international recognition.

Troubles were not over for Albania, however. Internal conflict; a period of rule by Italy; and, most difficult of all, Communist control followed. In 1944 Enver Hoxha was installed as leader. This new regime introduced severe political oppression. All political parties except the Communist Party were outlawed. The press, institutions, and organizations operated under tight controls. Few foreigners could enter the country, and only the party officials were permitted to travel outside the country. In 1967 all religious bodies were banned, Christian and Muslim church property was seized, and the country was declared the world's first atheist state. Christians experienced harsh persecution, and churches and mosques were bulldozed into the ground. The work Paul had begun almost 2,000 years before seemed to be defeated.

NEW GROWTH SHOOTS UP

We began the story of Albania with the thought that a woman, Lydia, perhaps played a part in getting Paul to Illyria, later Albania. We can know with assurance, however, that a woman was instrumental in Christians' second entry into Albania. In 1986, Mary Carpenter and her attorney husband, David, were serving in the First Baptist Church, Lake Brownwood (Tex.), as Mission Service Corps volunteers. Desiring to start the members of their little church in praying for missions, they called the Foreign Mission Board (FMB; now the International Mission Board) and requested the name of a specific country for which they could begin to pray. They received the name of Albania. Within their home, Mary and David committed themselves not only to pray but also to learn about this country of Albania. Their 4-year-old son led the family in their project, praying for Albania every night.

Later they returned to their home church, First Baptist Church in Brownwood, and discovered that in response to a request to the FMB, they, too, had received the country of Albania as a prayer focus. "Do you suppose they are giving this name to every church which calls?" they wondered. "Or is God telling our family something?"

Shortly after that, David confided that he felt perhaps God was calling them to go to Albania, and with Mary's agreement, he made his first contact with the FMB. "To Albania? You know no American has been allowed into that country for decades. Did you say you're a lawyer?" A strange request, but finally someone who understood their hearts, David Garrison, not only contacted them but also encouraged them in their call.

The Carpenters wanted to be ready when Albania opened up, and they were confident it would. The next step required that they sell their house and business and move to Fort Worth for a year's seminary training. They sold their house—by video— to a coach who was moving there. An Episcopalian lawyer from Houston approached David, wanting to buy his title company and law practice. "I don't know if you will understand this or not," he said, "but we just feel that God wants us to move here." The practice had not even been listed for sale.

Following the year at the seminary, the Carpenters were scheduled to move to a city nearby but not in Albania since they would not be allowed to live in the country. There they would have opportunities to network with other Christians in seeking ways to get the gospel inside Albania. A month before they were to leave for Albania, they received a call from the FMB. "It's open. You can go to Albania!"

As Communist rule in Eastern Europe collapsed in 1989 and in response to growing unrest and public protests, Ramiz Alia, then the first secretary of the Communist Party in Albania, restored religious freedom and made other governmental reforms. Several hard-line Communist leaders were removed. In the midst of demonstrations and general strikes, a coalition government was formed in June 1991, and collapsed in December. An interim administration was appointed, and elections were held in March 1992, giving the Democrats 92 of the 140 seats.

Into this milieu David and Mary moved with three children in September 1992. As the first foreigners to live there in many years, their survival skills were tested to the max by the scarcity of food and poor living conditions as they spent the first months learning the language and culture. Soon they began to realize that, while missionaries usually live in the cities, 70 percent of the population lived in the villages, and no one was attempting to reach them. But how was it possible? Most of the villages were remotely located and extremely difficult to enter.

In June 1993 Mary set up a meeting in a restaurant with three leaders of Campus Crusade for Christ (CCC). She provided the agenda, relating how God had placed in their hearts a real burden to reach the country. According to her plan, they would need the 50 Albanian students who had become Christians through the ministry of CCC, many outside volunteers, and long-term church planters from Baptist churches in the US. To Mary's amazement, Don Mansfield, leader of the Albanian CCC team, reached into his briefcase and pulled out a ten-page plan for what she had described. His plan lacked one thing Mary knew they could provide: a long-term church planting strategy. They had a match!

A Swiss helicopter team serving in the country for some time doing relief work longed to be involved in church planting. They became the third partner in the plan. Now it remained for Mary to "sell" it to their FMB supervisors. In spite their lack of missionary experience, Carpenter's plan was approved. They had a year to recruit 200 volunteers.

They sent in specific job requests, and people began to respond. By April 1994 the 12 ISC volunteers (those who had agreed to stay 2 years) were committed and would arrive in June, just weeks before the short-term volunteers would arrive on the field. Baptist Men organizations from many different states took the lead in manning the base camps. In addition to the work among Baptists, the staff of CCC enlisted volunteers as well, and the volunteers came!

The plan involved taking the volunteers to base camps where they received training in using Campus Crusade for Christ's *Jesus* film as an evangelism tool. Each team was comprised of four Westerners and two Albanian Christians who would travel to a village by means of a Land Rover, helicopter, or donkey, depending upon the village's accessibility. Teams became guests of the Albanian villagers, eating what they offered and when necessary, spending the night in accommodations they provided. Every team member knew that the chances for dysentery were high, but it never deterred them from their task.

Over the next three summers, the projects continued. Hundreds became Christians. Early in 1997, several fraudulent investment schemes in the country became evident, and thousands of Albanians lost their savings. Although the government promised partial reimbursement to many investors, the general populace had grown weary of the graft and scandal. Albanians in several cities began first to protest and then to riot. By March rebellion had broken out and parts of the country were virtually ungoverned. Local militias, armed citizens, defended themselves from looters in the southern part of the country.

DANGER IN THE FIELD

A number of Baptist missionaries were by now located in Albania, many of whom were living in vulnerable areas. Albanian Christians urged Debbie and Bert Ayers to leave because of the rebellion. In talking with fellow missionaries, they determined it wise to exit the country through Shkoder to the north, traveling through Montenegro to Bari, Italy. Painfully they took leave of their Albanian friends and church members. When would they see each other again? As they were leaving their Albanian home, accompanied by a Mennonite missionary family, they learned that in Shkoder 4 had been killed, 28 injured, and the entire area was out of control.

They heard further reports of increased violence. The Ayerses revised their plan and determined to go to Durres where they could take a ferry to Italy. All along the way, the Albanian military offered them weapons, but each time they refused. Upon arrival at the gate to the port in Durres, they communicated by radio to those already at the port. The prospects looked good; their missionary friends were hopeful the ferry would arrive in the afternoon. However, they would probably be permitted to take only one small bag with them.

Bert left to find a friend with whom they could leave the van, and Debbie was to repack their bag.

68

Suddenly, she felt as if she had been hit on the head by a cast-iron skillet and fell to the ground. Bert arrived quickly at her side and determined she had been shot. Quickly putting Debbie in a car, they asked an Albanian man standing by where the hospital was located. He agreed to go with them and give directions. In retrospect both Debbie and Bert acknowledged how strange it was that the shooting did not attract a large crowd as it normally would. Only this lone Albanian stood by.

"Go this way," said the Albanian "Turn here!"

"But it's not a road," answered Bert. By following the directions, however, they were able to arrive at the hospital much more quickly. When the missionary who had driven them to the hospital returned to the ferry port gate and turned to thank his guide, the Albanian was nowhere to be seen. He had just disappeared. Debbie is convinced God sent them an angel in their extreme situation.

Later that evening, after Debbie had received the care the local hospital could provide, they returned to the port gate and were joyfully reunited with their children and friends. They were very cognizant of God's protection as other near misses of gunfire continued among the crowd gathered there awaiting rescue. Late in the evening an Italian boat arrived. The Italian Marines tried to control the large crowd which had gathered, but to little avail. An Italian diplomat pulled Debbie and two of the children onto a boat, leaving Bert and the other two children behind. Only the next morning did Debbie learn Bert and the children had boarded a later boat and were safe as well.

In order to stop the rioting and murder, the president of Albania agreed to hold general elections in June and to resign if his party lost. International forces came to protect the people, but they were only mandated to see that humanitarian assistance be delivered to the areas that desperately needed it.

The Socialists with 65 percent of the votes won the elections that month. The Democrats mustered only 19 percent, and as a result, they boycotted parliament for the rest of the year and into 1998. In the summer of 1997 the *Jesus* film project to the villages by the Baptist and CCC teams had to be called off.

In the summer of 1998, however, the project continued, but instead of 300 Westerners and a small band of Albanians, the tables were turned. Now Albanians held all leadership positions, and the volunteers numbered 350. Only 50 people from outside Albania assisted.

Relations with Yugoslavia became worse because of the killing of several Serbian police officials by ethnic Albanians in Kosovo. The killings resulted in a brutal crackdown by Serbian authorities, and Albanian officials feared a flood of refugees from Kosovo. Their fears were not misplaced. Countless numbers of Kosovo refugees did indeed flood Albania that year.

By the summer of 1999, the joint project of Baptists and CCC, now named Project Aero, became an outreach tool for Kosovo refugees. According to an email report to the Carpenters from Don Mansfield, the teams were in 30 refugee camps, 137 Albanian villages, and 6 Kosovar cities. More than 280 Albanians participated. According to Mansfield, most Albanian believers feel that Aero is the best thing evangelistically that has ever happened to the country.

THE MATURING OF THE BODY
Who are these Albanian Christians who in spite of great difficulties are faithful to God? What causes

70

them to reach out in compassion to the refugees and their great need? They are the common people who have suffered and thus know how to serve others who suffer. They are also people of some note, like Mira, the young woman who administers the Baptist Union of Albania, of the Baptist World Alliance. Active in her church, she assists in the worship service, sings with the youth choir, and translates for English-speaking guests. Oh, by the way: Mira is also a medical doctor and serves as the only medical professional in a health center where the roster of patients includes many refugees. Mira's medical training includes several specialties, qualifying her to well-paid positions all over the world, but she believes God wants her to serve Him in Albania.

When Mary and David relate the events of their service in Albania, prayer is the dominant theme. Out of their prayers and those of others, a massive movement of Christ in Albania began to reawaken the Church. Paul must rejoice in heaven to see the cooperative efforts of Christians that have built up the Church again. I cannot help but believe Lydia is on the front row of a huge crowd of witnesses cheering on the saints in Albania.

Our Part in the Harvest

No doubt many Americans were unable to believe that the most atheistic country in the world could be reclaimed for Christ; but those who did, rejoice in the Lord's harvest there. Thank God that a few of His children see beyond the impossible to victory.

Today we are aware of many other countries in our world that are difficult to penetrate with the gospel. Because of strong religious beliefs or political philosophies, their governments restrict the freedom of religion we hold dear. Planting of the seed requires new approaches and innovative strategies. Pray daily for those who stand ready for the first open door, as Mary and David Carpenter did. Pray for those missionaries who risk their very lives, as did Debbie and Bert Ayers.

If your church does not pray for an unreached people group, suggest this project to your pastor or missions committee. As you pray, learn all you can about these people. Ask God to allow your church to experience the opening of doors to the gospel. And don't be surprised if in this exercise God is preparing you to answer your own prayers. Stranger things have happened.

6

Right Time, Right Place

A rather new phenomenon in our time is the emergence of shopping outlets. In the beginning the merchandise resulted from overruns and "seconds." Today we have the sneaky suspicion that these stores and their products were deliberately created for the bargain mind-set of today's shopper.

During World War II, scarcity of certain items was a fact of life: tires, gasoline, shoes, and, more importantly, chocolate, bubble gum, and other "goodies." When one of us children happened into a store where a small shipment of one of these items had been placed on the shelves, great was the rejoicing! In order to find these valued products you had to be in the right place at the right time. My husband, Bill, being a budding child entrepreneur, usually chose to save some of his cache to sell to friends not so fortunate as he. Penny gum would bring 50 cents, not a bad markup—for the seller!

All of us understand the principle of being in the right place at the right time. One story in the Bible illustrates it perhaps better than any other. You will find it in Acts 8:26–39.

After the martyrdom of Stephen, the persecution of Christians became more and more heated. The refugees who were driven from Jerusalem by the persecution of Saul refused, however, to allow the disaster to end their witness to Christ.

Philip, one of the seven deacons chosen to care for the Hellenist widows in Jerusalem along with Stephen, moved to Samaria. Many people of Israelite origin but with a mixture of Gentile blood lived there. Like Stephen, Philip was chosen as a deacon but soon became an effective evangelist. Philip not only declared God's words, he also performed miracles with God's power. As a result, many converted to Christianity.

Philip was sensitive to God's leadership, so he probably was not surprised when an angel appeared to him and said, "'Get up and go toward the south to the road that goes down from Jerusalem to Gaza.'" (Acts 8:26 NRSV) Unlike most of us, who would have wanted to know why and to be given more specific directions, Stephen "got up and went." The Lord honored his unquestioning obedience while he was on the way.

Philip met an Ethiopian eunuch who was returning in his chariot from Jerusalem where he had been worshiping. The eunuch was minister over the treasury of Candace, the queen of Ethiopia. Although he had gone to Jerusalem to worship, as a eunuch he could never have any hope in participating fully in the worship of God with the Jews (Deut. 23:1). He could not even enter the congregation of the Jews, according to Old Testament law. However, here in God's open spaces, such exclusion did not matter. Philip was about to give him the opportunity through faith in Christ to enter the congregation of the new Israel of God.

Just in case Philip did not understand his task, the angel said, "'Go over to this chariot and join it'" (Acts 8:29). So eager was Philip to follow his orders that he ran to the chariot. Perhaps he was surprised to hear the Ethiopian reading a passage from the 53rd chapter of Isaiah.

"Do you understand what you are reading?" Philip asked.

"'How can I, unless someone guides me?'" the eunuch responded. How could Philip have asked for a more open invitation? He took this Old Testament passage and told him the good news of salvation in Christ.

Philip must have spoken of baptism, for as they passed an area of water, the eunuch said, "'Here is water. What is to prevent me from being baptized?" Could it be that he had fear of another exclusionary matter? He commanded the chariot be stopped, and he and Philip went down into the water. What a glorious time that must have been!

The chapter ends with Philip's being caught up by the Spirit of the Lord and the Ethiopian continuing his journey with rejoicing. Right place, right time for the planting of a new believer in another part of the world. What if Philip had been slow to respond? We often hear of a "narrow window of opportunity." Philip's immediate obedience enabled God's good news to be spread to the uttermost.

MODERN-DAY PHILIP

A team from Campus Crusade in northern Iraq might have felt like Philip meeting with the Ethiopian eunuch, but without an angelic directive, some time ago. They had gone to this country to distribute Bibles and copies of the *Jesus* film. On one occasion they had loaded Bibles into their vehicle and set out for a village some distance away.

Suddenly, and without warning, the vehicle stalled, locked up, and would not start. Not knowing what else to do, the team left the vehicle and began walking. After they had gone only a short distance, they saw a man squatting by the road. As they approached him, he said, "I have been waiting for you. Where are the Bibles?"

The Bibles still in the car were not earmarked for any special persons, so the team returned to the vehicle and joyfully turned them over to the man. When asked about how he knew they were coming with Bibles, he responded, "I had a vision that someone was coming to share the good news with my village."

That is not the end of the story. When the man went happily on his way, the driver tried once again to start the vehicle. Yes, you would believe that it started immediately, transporting them to their next rendezvous with seekers.

RIGHT TIME, RIGHT PLACE IN BOLIVIA

Time and again, God has demonstrated His power in providing answers to problems, cures for ills, and relief to the suffering—all in the nick of time.

For one woman, the right time occurred in the summer of 1999 and the right place was her village of La Merced, home to an indigenous people group dating back to 1,600 years before Christ. For some months she had anticipated the birth of her child, but because hospitals were far away, they almost never figured into a birth event in her village. Even if a hospital were located nearby, they could never save enough money to cover the cost of its services. They would just have to rely on the resources of the village when the time came for the baby to arrive.

Unfortunately, the baby did not wait for the expected arrival time. Weeks before the due date, the young woman began to experience labor pains. Her mother and other women of the village tenderly ministered to her needs, treating her with medicines made of roots and herbs to diminish the discomfort and rubbing her abdomen with oil. As time went on, the contractions grew more intense and painful and the woman began to hemorrhage.

Meanwhile, a medical team from Brookwood Baptist Church in Birmingham, Alabama, was hard at work in a clinic in another part of La Merced. The team included Dr. Frank Page, an outstanding obstetrician, not a novice at practicing medicine in villages like La Merced. He had given time out of a busy practice on two other occasions for a medical missions trip to Venezuela. While he had gained a fine reputation in his field in the US, he had become accustomed to working without the sophisticated equipment found in his Birmingham office and hospital in places like this. His nurse, Becca, and daughter, Elise, assisted him in the La Merced clinic.

Suddenly, a man ran into the clinic saying his wife was having trouble delivering a baby. Fearing for her life and the life of his baby, he sought the help of the foreign doctors. When Page saw the woman, he recognized a very serious complication. Not only was the baby premature, it was breach as well.

The team's translator, Jo, and a dentist named Steve joined them in the small dark room. Page instructed everyone on the importance of remaining calm and following directions. When the baby was born, after making sure the baby was stable, Page went to work to help the mother. She had lost much blood and had a third-degree laceration from the difficult birth. He explained to the little group that they must get the baby warm and put him on his mother's breast. Nursing became a critical treatment, for it prompts contractions of the uterus, and without this intervention this mother would continue to hemorrhage.

With an IV hanging on a nail in the wall, Page was able to stabilize the woman enough to load her on a truck to be transported to a school where he could suture the laceration. Because Page was in Bolivia, not the US, specifically in this small village at the right time, mother and baby survived this difficult ordeal.

How does Frank Page describe the situation? "So many of us have wonderful fulfillment in our careers, but things like this add ultimate meaning to our careers. This may be one of the most significant deliveries I have done."

The next day Page and Mike Royer, an anchorman for a local TV affiliate in Birmingham who went along to report the trip, went back to check on mother and baby. Royer reported, "It seems that yesterday was her special day, the day of the most difficult birth, the day that one of the best doctors in America was just up the street."

TIME, PLACE—HOW DO WE KNOW IT IS RIGHT?

While an angel generally told Philip the time and place of his opportunity, most of us rely on less direct instruction. This was the case for Bill and me in July 1963.

Only 5 months before, we had left family and friends to serve God as missionaries in Indonesia. The day before we departed we had received the doctor's confirmation that I was pregnant with child number three. His announcement brought a mixture of joy and consternation. While we were thrilled with the thought of another baby, my history with having babies was not good.

We had lost our second child, a girl, in the seventh month. With Erin, the next child, I threatened premature delivery and spent the last 2 months in bed. No cause for either complication had been diagnosed. What if this misfortune was repeated in Indonesia? Was the medical care in that country adequate?

We spent 4 months in the Philippines, awaiting a visa to enter Indonesia. When our visa arrived in June, we again faced a decision. Should we go immediately or wait until the baby came in November? We chose to leave at once.

We had no way of knowing that one of the Mission doctors in Indonesia had had a great deal of experience with my medical problem, known now to be an incompetent cervix. In fact, he had developed a procedure for the condition that was not yet being used in the US. When premature labor began in July, I rode for several hours over rough roads in the back seat of a jeep to the Baptist Hospital in East Java. There Ralph Bethea saved the life of our son, Ross. Three and a half months later he was born a healthy, full-term baby, after a normal delivery.

On our home assignment 3 years later, my Dallas obstetrician, a deacon in our church, mused over this event. "You are very fortunate. Had you been here in Dallas, we could not have saved your baby. We had not developed that specialized procedure."

Right time, right place for us was on the island of Java, Indonesia, at the birth of our son. When new missionaries wonder about the risks of living overseas, I tell them this story. No place on earth can offer the assurance of health and safety like being where God has called you.

Your Right Time and Place

Being fortunate enough to be in the right place at the right time once does not assure that we will be exempt from the opposite. How can we know when we have no visible instruction?

Of course, nothing provides more help than prayer. When we verbalize our needs, God brings clarification and direction. Give time to being quiet and pondering the situation, allowing the Holy Spirit opportunity to speak.

Trust your feelings. If God has truly had the opportunity to speak, even though not audibly, trust your instincts. Search the Scriptures for verses that might apply. Discuss it with a trusted, Christian friend. Philip only had scant information as to his mission, but he acted on what he had in hand. Almost never do we have all the facts, requiring that we trust the Holy Spirit's urgings.

A consistently open heart to God's work places one in unexpected situations. Just today I received an email from a friend, a director of an associational Christian Women's Job Corps®. One of their clients, mother of a 22-month-old baby, has just disappeared, apparently back on drugs. If she does not return today, authorities will place her baby in foster care and she will lose her place in the shelter. Few of us would claim the wisdom to advise this CWJC℠ leader, but God will guide her in just the right direction at just the right time. She has been placed there for such a time as this. Having His wisdom in every circumstance is one of the awesome gifts of God.

7

Upon His Word

*I*f you had an offer of the world's best counseling service and you could get it free, would you take it? If you could trust a news source to be truthful and reliable, would you subscribe to it? If you were offered a series of letters containing a gift of pure love and acceptance, would you read them? If you were told that you already had these phenomenal treasures in your home, would you believe it?

Many Americans have at least one Bible in their home, but they never open it. It sits ignored on a table or gathers dust on a bookshelf. Yet it contains everything the above paragraph describes—and more!

Knowing the Bible is a best-seller and an excellent piece of literature may prove reason enough for some people to buy it, but it takes intentionality, discipline, and commitment from the reader for the Bible to become a best-read book. More than just a collection of wise sayings and interesting events, the Bible was written as a holy book, the Word of God. The writer of Hebrews gives evidence to his experience in interacting with the holy God through Scripture: "For the word of God is living and active. Sharper than any double-edged sword, it penetrates even to dividing soul and spirit, joints and marrow;

it judges the thoughts and attitudes of the heart"
(Heb. 4:12 NIV).

One cannot read the Scriptures in the power of
the Holy Spirit and not examine and sometimes
change attitudes, values, and motives. The Bible is a
powerful book!

THE POWER OF THE WORD IN THE OLD TESTAMENT

Just suppose the Bible had been hidden away for
years. Imagine that no one had ever seen a copy, and
no one ever even referred to it. While it is hard for us
even to imagine this scenario, this was the situation
when Josiah came to the throne of Judah around 640
B.C. (2 Kings 22).

Josiah was crowned king as a child, only 8 years
old. His father, Amon, had been on the throne only
2 years when government officials engaged in a plot
to assassinate him. His murder in the palace itself
incensed the people loyal to Amon, and after a countercoup in which the enemies of the king were killed,
little Josiah was named king.

Poor Josiah! How could a mere child have the
wisdom to reign in such a turbulent time? Easy: God
gave it to him. Although his father, Amon, and his
grandfather, Manasseh, had both done evil in the
sight of the Lord, Josiah spent his 31 years on the
throne modeling the reign of David. We do not
know who or what set Josiah on a quest for God, but
when he had been king for 8 years, he began to seek
Him. Four years later he became convicted to purge
Judah and Jerusalem of all altars of heathen worship,
and this he did with a vengeance (2 Chron. 34:1–7).

In the 18th year of Josiah's reign, he gave instructions to his men to go to the temple of the Lord. "Go
to Hilkiah, the high priest," he said, "and tell him to

take the money that has been collected from the temple doorkeepers and buy the necessary materials to hire carpenters, builders, and masons to clean and repair the temple" (2 Kings 22:4–5, *paraphrase*).

As they were bringing out the money that had been taken into the temple of the Lord, Hilkiah found a book. He knew its importance immediately. As he placed it in the hands of Shaphan, Josiah's secretary, he quietly communicated the significance of his discovery: "'I have found the book of the law in the house of the Lord'" (2 Kings 22:8 NRSV).

When Shaphan returned to King Josiah, he first reported on the progress of the repairs. "Your workers are doing everything that has been committed to them. They have paid out the money and entrusted it to the supervisors and workers, just as you have ordered." Then Shaphan added, "'The priest Hilkiah has given me a book'" (2 Kings 22:10 NRSV).

"A book? What kind of a book? What does it say?" *(Paraphrased.)*

When the king heard the words of the book of the law, he tore his robes. Could it be that the portion of Deuteronomy he heard that day was: "After you have had children and grandchildren and have lived in the land a long time—if then you become corrupt and make any kind of an idol, doing evil in the eyes of the Lord your God and provoking him to anger, I call heaven and earth as witnesses against you this day that you will quickly perish from the land you are crossing the Jordan to possess. You will not live there long but will certainly be destroyed" (Deut. 4:25–26 NIV).

Whatever passage of that book he read, it was enough to frighten him to instant action. Josiah sent Hilkiah, Shaphan and his son, and two others to consult with the prophetess Huldah.

"'Go and inquire of the Lord for me and for the people and for all Judah about what is written in this book that has been found. Great is the Lord's anger that burns against us because our fathers have not obeyed the words of this book; they have not acted in accordance with all that is written there concerning us'" (2 Kings 22:13 NIV).

Josiah must have paced the floor, awaiting God's verdict. The message was clear; the sins of his people were bound to be their undoing. Justice called for the promised consequences. If they had only known of this book earlier!

When Hilkiah's group returned, they brought good news and bad news. The bad news was that destruction could not be avoided because the people had forsaken God, made idols, and worshiped false gods. The good news was that because Josiah had humbled himself before God and had wept in bitter repentance, he would not see the disaster that would come. He would die in peace.

Shortly afterward, Josiah sent out a call for all the inhabitants of Judah and Jerusalem and all the priests and prophets to come to the house of the Lord. In their presence he read the book of the covenant that had been found, and in a prominent place he promised before the Lord to walk after Him and keep His commandments with all his heart and soul. Then all the people joined in the covenant.

The profound experience of finding anew the word of the Lord changed an entire nation. They burned vessels used in the worship of Baal, tore down altars to false gods, and removed false priests and female cult prostitutes. The people came together in the celebration of the Passover, symbolizing their return to God. Josiah was remembered for his leadership, led by the God Who is always true to

His Word. "Before him there was no king like him, who turned to the Lord with all his heart, with all his soul, and with all his might, according to all the law of Moses; nor did any like him arise after him" (2 Kings 23:25 NRSV).

The miraculous power of God's Holy Word! Those of us who have known the Scriptures, having had it read to us before we could even recognize the letters on the page, too often take the written Word for granted. For those who read the Scriptures for the first time later in life, it truly becomes like "a double-edged sword."

The Power of God's Word Today

In Vietnam

During the war in Vietnam, thousands of people moved out of the heavy fighting in the highlands to relative security of the coastal plain. Mr. and Mrs. Le Huynh Mai, American missionaries given these names by the Vietnamese, went to this area to begin churches. While they served there, a Baptist woman and member of one of these churches died. Her husband wanted her to be buried in the family burial grounds outside her home village. Reverend Mai agreed to go for the service, even though he would be conducting it in a place where ancestor worship was prominent. Additionally, the area lay dangerously close to the insecure highlands.

Mai's commitment to give the family, and the whole village, a message of eternal life was affirmed when after the service the village chief asked him to leave the "book" with them so they could read more from it. This one copy would serve the whole village.

In the days immediately following, security risks made it impossible for Mai to return to this village. Finally, after three months, the situation eased temporarily, and Mai returned to find a small group of believers meeting regularly and discussing the Bible. No preacher, no teacher. The Word spoke for itself in the hearts of those moved by the Spirit to claim it.

In Russia
While the miracle that occurred during Josiah's reign has never been replicated on a national level, the dramatic change in lives today simply as a result of reading the Scriptures is likewise astonishing. When we realize the power of God's Holy Book, how can we neglect the distribution of Bibles worldwide?

In September 1983, Moscow, Russia, hosted the International Book Fair. Large New York publishers refused to go unless all publishers, including religious publishers, could participate. Johnnie Godwin, along with a few colleagues, represented Southern Baptist's Broadman and Holman Publishers. Because the fair was held just three days after Russia shot down a Korean Air jet, the foreign publishers walked into a very tense situation. While Johnnie and the others could exhibit their religious material, they could not give out or sell Bibles with the exception of a few marked with the inscription, For Research. Clearly the Iron Curtain was not open to any religious expression.

Four years later, Moscow hosted the International Book Fair once again. Although *glasnost* (openness) and *perestroika* (restructuring) were emerging, it was still impossible to sell Bibles, and even difficult to carry personal copies for one's own use.

In 1989, however, because of the completely different climate, the Evangelical Christian Publishers

Association (ECPA), of which Johnnie was a board member, took 10,000 Russian New Testaments into Moscow with permission to distribute them only within the fairground building itself. People flocked to the Bible exhibit to obtain their own copies. Exhibitors periodically closed down the distribution in order to gain some semblance of order. Meanwhile, the crowd grew for the next opportunity to get a New Testament. The KGB (state secret police) helped to keep the crowd organized—a new role for them!

That same year Madalyn Murray O'Hair hosted an American Atheist Press booth immediately adjacent to the Bible distribution site. At one point Johnnie asked one man in line to receive a New Testament why he did not leave that line and go to the next booth where no one waited to get material on atheism. "We've tried that before," the man replied emotionally. "I want a Bible."

In 1991, because of the openness to God's Word, Johnnie led the ECPA to raise money to take 4 million Bibles, enough to place a New Testament into every home in Moscow. Many publishers and denominations were involved in the project. A Baptist Young Women Enterprisers group representing WMU went to Moscow to help in the distribution of Bibles. The week before they were to leave, the Communists attempted a coup in Moscow, but within 24 hours the attempt failed, leaving the city even more open. What had been feared had indeed been used of God for good.

Hungry for the Word of God, people willingly stood in long lines to get their copies of the Bible. After receiving their copies, they often pressed them to their chests, walked away a few steps, and began reading voraciously. Others, attracted by the crowds, expressed curiosity about this book they had never even seen, let alone read.

Early in the tour, the group left their bus at a Moscow corner eager to share the gospel even in the rain. A tall college student immediately approached Andrea Mullins, leader of the group. "What are you doing here?" he asked. To Andrea's surprise he spoke English fluently.

Andrea responded to his question with another. "Are you familiar with the Bible?" His puzzled expression told her he did not know about the book she was holding in her hand. She opened one of the Russian New Testaments they were giving away to John 3:16 and asked if he could translate the Russian into English. Slowly, with her help, the young man read, for the first time, this beloved verse proclaiming God's love. Andrea told him of Jesus, God's Son, and of the sacrifice that God had made for him. "I have come all the way from America to tell you that God loves you." He was stunned to hear that Andrea had come all those many miles just to let him know of God's great love for him.

Andrea continued to point out Scriptures underscoring the marvelous grace of God and His desire to offer salvation to him. Finally, she asked, "Would you like to have a personal relationship with God?" He answered with a strong "Yes," and there on the street corner, he prayed the believer's prayer and gave his life to Christ.

When Andrea handed him the Russian New Testament, the young man said, "I am going to read this Bible to my wife and daughter so they can know Jesus, too." What if the Enterprisers group had listened to concerned friends and not gone to Moscow because of the possible risks? Perhaps this man would never have heard—or someone else would have had the joy of leading him to Christ.

On one of the days the group was in Russia, Andrea and Deborah Brunt held a worship service, right in the middle of Red Square. They took turns standing on a makeshift podium, a box of Russian New Testaments, as they told those who gathered around, through an interpreter, of God's love revealed through Christ. As they spoke, the crowd grew larger and larger. Many who had been standing in a line to visit Lenin's Tomb left that line to see what the foreign women were saying. At the close, Andrea and Deborah offered a Bible and an accompanying tract to help them know more about God. The response was overwhelming! As the crowd pressed forward, the women tried to speak to each one, but the crowd was too large. Most left with the tract and Bible and many prayers that God's Word would reap a great harvest.

Jimmie Chappell, another member of the group, had spent hours handing out Bibles on the crowded street, traveling far down the plaza area of Arbot Street. When she glanced at her watch, she noted that it was past time to return to the bus. She offered the remaining Bibles in her bag to a group of people who gladly took them. Pleased with the accomplishments of the day, Jimmie turned to retrace her steps up the plaza, when she almost ran over a little Russian woman, a *babushka*. Jimmie had not noticed her but realized the woman had been watching her for some time. With her hands held out toward Jimmie, she pled, "Biblia?" Jimmie shook her head; none were left.

"Biblia! Biblia!" Her cries were more emphatic now. "Nyet," Jimmie reiterated, opening her bag to show her none were inside. Still she cried, "Biblia! Biblia!"

By this time, Jimmie was trembling with emotion and frustration. She remembered the words of one their leaders: "You will never have enough Scriptures. If you have 100, you need 200. If you have 10,000 you need 20,000. If you have 1 million, you need 2 million." But Jimmie only needed 1. Impulsively, she took the babushka by her hand and dragged her up the plaza. Surely, someone would have a Bible left over from the day's distribution.

As she was reunited with her group, she went from one to another until at last she found one lone copy. With joy she turned to give the precious book to the woman, when out of the blue a younger woman materialized and grabbed tightly to the other end of the Bible. For an endless few seconds they stood toe to toe, playing tug of war with the Bible. Jimmie jerked, the young woman jerked, and in the background the little babushka cried, "Biblia! Biblia!"

A cry tore from Jimmie's heart. "Lord, I can't make this choice!" The response burned its way into her very soul, "Jimmie, you make this choice every day; you just do not see it."

Jimmie had to do something. She had to choose. She jerked the New Testament out of the hands of the young woman and gave it to the little babushka. And then the celebration began. The old woman raised her voice and beat the Bible against her chest. She kissed the precious book, and then she hugged and kissed Jimmie. It was a glorious moment.

As soon as Jimmie could pull away from her, she turned back to find the young woman. She had disappeared into the crowd.

The week, filled with similar events, was soon over. The group reluctantly boarded the bus to return to the Moscow airport where it had all started. Andrea was waiting in line to have her passport checked when she noticed the uniformed woman checking the passports. She was a large woman with a scowl on her face, and Andrea felt a shiver of fear down her spine.

"Give her a New Testament," the Spirit whispered. But Andrea only saw a woman who appeared disinterested, and she had to confess that she was afraid. As she struggled with this Spirit-directed order, she realized she was the only one left in the room who still had Bibles. What should she do?

Drawing on all her courage and the Holy Spirit's strength, Andrea broke into the long line in front of the woman military officer, and meekly said, "Biblia?" The woman took the Bible and began to look at it, but because she was seated at a desk, Andrea could not see her face. She was able to see that the woman would read a little and then turn a few pages. When she stood and looked at Andrea, tears were streaming down her cheeks, and then she embraced Andrea, saying, "Thank you! Thank you!" in Russian. She raised her arms in praise to God and went from soldier to soldier in the room, reading passages from the pages, tears constantly flowing. Andrea confessed, "What I had mistaken as a woman disinterested in God, a woman of mean spirit, was in truth one of God's children, hungering for His Word in a dry and thirsty land."

In Your Life
Stories of the effectiveness of God's Word in bringing light to the life abound. Do you know the supreme joy of sharing this message with another? If not, try giving the Word of God away. It's a message of love and salvation to all.

You can always give Bibles to friends on special occasions. Be sure to select a translation which matches the level of reading and understanding of the person for whom you purchase it. Religious books, carefully selected to communicate the message of the gospel effectively, also make appropriate gifts. By doing these things, you tell your friend that you value God's Word, that it holds importance in your life. Point out special passages especially meaningful to you in your daily walk. Discuss questions she may have as a result of her reading. Pray that the Holy Spirit will create a hunger for the Word and enlighten her eyes for understanding.

When you travel, or even as you just move around in your hometown, carry a new Bible or portions of the Scriptures to give away. Pray in advance for those who will receive them. Marked passages will provide assistance in finding special verses for witnessing opportunity. When you go to your doctor's office, leave a Bible or Scripture portion behind for others to read.

The American Bible Society (ABS) exists to distribute God's Word throughout our nation. Write to discover ways you can be involved in this ministry (1865 Broadway, New York, NY 10023; or visit their Web site at www.americanbible.org). The ABS partnered with WMU in the preparation of a special edition of the *Contemporary English Version* of the Bible for clients of Christian Women's Job Corps.

Most important of all, read God's Word daily. Let your children see you spend time studying its pages. Discuss your readings with your spouse, a friend, or your children. You will find it feeds the soul. Never underestimate the power of God's Word. After all, it is the Living Word.

8

Treading on Snakes and Scorpions

*H*ave you ever wondered why missionaries choose to go into dangerous places to take the gospel? What is more curious, why do they choose to stay there? People in many safe countries of the world need the gospel too. Why put yourself and your family at risk? American suburbs are full of people who do not follow Christ. Why would anyone submit herself to the dangers of criminals and drug addicts?

If you use Prayer Patterns[1] to guide you in praying by name for missionaries on their birthdays, every day you see a tiny cross with the words, *Last Frontier Missionaries.* We cannot see the names of these missionaries or their locations because they live in areas of the world hostile to the good news of Christ. Even printing their names invites danger to them. Others listed by name risk their very lives in countries without adequate health facilities or in areas of drug trafficking. Even in our own country, missionaries put their lives on the line every day in areas where drive-by shootings and gang activity are commonplace. Does God really expect that kind of sacrifice?

Toward the end of Jesus' ministry on earth, He sent out 70 of His choice followers not exactly to the ends of the earth, but certainly to unfamiliar territory. He "sent them on ahead in pairs to every town and place where he himself intended to go" (Luke 10:1 NRSV). When this evangelistic mission returned, they were ecstatic. "Lord, in your name even the demons submit to us." No wonder they were full of joy! It seemed they were invincible. Jesus reminded them, "'See, I have given you authority to tread on snakes and scorpions, and over all the power of the enemy; and nothing will hurt you'" (10:19). Do you remember Paul's experience with a snake? You will find it in Acts 27:39 to 28:6.

TREADING ON A SNAKE ON MALTA

The natives of Malta had awakened early in the morning to see the ship drifting nearby, obviously seeking a harbor. They watched as the strangers neared the bay, not an altogether good choice, for the bay contained a shoal, a sandbar hidden by high tide, which had caused unknowing navigators great difficulty. Sure enough, the bow of the ship struck the mud bank, the heavy surf broke the stern of the ship, and the rough waters shattered the ship before their very eyes.

The Maltese watched as one by one the 276 passengers jumped overboard and headed for the beach. Amazingly, not one person failed to make it ashore.

The natives, seeing these wet and cold survivors, began gathering kindling on the beach for a fire. The man they called Paul immediately joined them in seeking wood and fanning the flames into a roaring fire.

One man saw the quick movement of the viper in the bundle Paul carried. The poisonous snake fastened its fangs into Paul's hand. Others joined the native's horrified gaze. "Surely this man is a murderer!" they thought. "He has offended our goddess of justice, and while he escaped the dangerous sea, he has finally gotten his due!"

Their eyes, along with those of the men from the ship, were fixed on Paul, expecting the poison from the snake to do its work, causing his hand to swell and bring about quick and certain death. Paul, however, quite unconcerned, merely tossed the snake into the fire as one might flick away an annoying fly.

The sailors and soldiers from the ship watched with horror. Julius, the centurion into whose hands Paul along with a few other prisoners had been entrusted, was especially anxious. Paul, as a Roman citizen, would plead his cause before Caesar upon their arrival. How could he explain the death of this notorious prisoner?

The sailors, too, had a vested interest in the life of this Paul. Had he not encouraged them all along this turbulent voyage? Too bad the centurion had not heeded Paul's advice to linger at Crete. They could have avoided this mishap.

"Sirs, I perceive that the voyage will be with injury and much loss, not only of the cargo and ship, but also of our lives," Paul had warned. Because the centurion listened instead to the captain of the ship, who had declared the harbor to be unsuitable, they had proceeded to another harbor 40 miles away for the winter.

Almost from the beginning they had rued this decision. Soon after setting sail, a northeaster struck down from the land and drove the ship into open sea. Tossed to and fro by the vicious winds, the sailors were forced to throw overboard cargo and even part of the ship's rigging. Their situation seemed hopeless.

Paul, knowing of the sense of desperation, went to the sailors. First he urged them to eat. Because of the unending work necessary to deal with the emergencies, they had not eaten and had become weak. Then he encouraged them to take heart. He told them that an angel of the God he worshiped had appeared to him saying they should not fear.

"Do not be afraid, Paul; you must stand before the emperor; and indeed, God has granted safety to all those who are sailing with you" (Acts 27:24 NRSV). His words gave courage to the sailors. They had come to depend on him, and now it seemed their mentor was facing death. Could it be that his God did not have the power to deliver him? If not, what of their own fate?

They continued to stare at Paul. They waited for a long time. When it became evident that Paul had miraculously escaped death, the natives believed he himself was a god. No ordinary man could have survived. Paul, although the Scripture does not directly say so, probably rejoiced in this new opportunity to tell of the powerful God he served.

TREADING ON SNAKES IN AFRICA

Almost 2,000 years later, John Dina was not on Malta, but in Mozambique, a long way from his home in Arizona. God had called him to serve with his wife, Wanne, and three children, Hannah, Andrew, and Matthew in the Zambezia Province as a general evangelist. On October 16, 1996, after having returned from stateside assignment in June, John consulted with three church leaders and a layman in the bush area near his home. Eighty churches had requested his assistance since June. They needed a plan for serving these churches.

As the men walked along the path, John felt what he thought was a thorn in his right calf. When he looked down more closely, he saw a bright, almost fluorescent green snake wriggling near a fallen tree where seconds before it had hidden unseen. As John and his friends inspected the single line of blood running down his calf, one of the men began to shout, "Run, brother, it's coming!"

Sure enough, when John turned around, the snake was literally coming straight at them. John did not take time to reason that this snake's behavior was certainly different from the rattlesnakes in Arizona, but discovered later that African snakes are much more aggressive and fast-moving than snakes in America. Fortunately, the men were able to outdistance this one.

When they were finally able to catch their breath, John noticed that the time on his watch was 2:30 P.M. John began to think about what Wanne might think of this venture. "Boy, I'd better not tell her about this. She would only worry." He himself rejoiced that the whole thing was over.

The other men, however, had more serious concerns. One began to run the blade of his pocketknife over the wound to see if the snake had left its fang over the puncture. Cautiously, they started the hike back to the truck.

John gives his description of this struggle: "In about 5 to 7 minutes I began to have difficulty speaking. I began to salivate like crazy, and a sensation of heat ran up my body; it was like walking into a Jacuzzi."

For John, holding on to one of the men, stopping to rest or vomit, the return trip to the truck was grueling. "My body was tingling all over like it feels when your arm goes to sleep, and my throat was tightening up like you feel when you are waking up after being put to sleep, hearing voices but indistinctly."

The Mozambicans, obviously afraid, made a circle around John and prayed for him. He asked one of his friends if the snakebite was usually deadly. "Oh, no," he responded. "It just makes you very sick," knowing he spoke an untruth to keep John from worrying. Actually his cousin had died from the same kind of snakebite when he had accidentally run over it and gotten it tangled up in the spokes of his bicycle.

Mamba is the common name for four venomous snakes in the cobra family found in tropical and southern Africa. All have narrow heads with relatively large eyes and are among the swiftest snakes in the world. So potent is their venom that if a person who has been bitten does not get treatment with antivenom, he will likely not survive.

John made the last distance to the truck carried in the arms of his friends. Even then the challenge to get home loomed over him. None of the other men could drive; John would have to do it himself. He would drive a few miles, stop the car to vomit, feel some better, and start the same cycle over again. After five hours the truck pulled into his drive.

The missions community, which included the International Mission Board (IMB) and World Vision, swung into action. Larry Randolph, fellow missionary, telephoned Barbara Curnutt, then director of women's missions and ministry for the Florida Baptist Convention. For some time, through a prayer partnership with Mozambique, the members of Woman's Missionary Union (WMU) had been charged with communicating prayer needs to the women in the churches. Larry's request for prayer for John was quickly relayed to the churches. Larry also asked Barbara to alert the IMB. Requests for prayer were also posted on the IMB's prayerline. Was it just a coincidence that John's name had been on the missionary prayer calendar on October 12?

IMB's Martha McAlister contacted a doctor in Johannesburg who specialized in snakes, and he advised that John be given steroids in preparation for antivenom. The next morning he was airlifted to Johannesburg and put in an intensive care unit. By then infection had caused his lower leg to swell. After treatment for four days, John's breathing had returned to normal, the swelling in the leg had gone down, and the tremor in his hands was gone.

John insists prayer is responsible for his recovery—prayers of the Mozambican men, fellow Christians around the world, and especially his wife, Wanne, who prayerfully supported him throughout the ordeal. They confidently tell friends and strangers alike that God used the event as one more way to show His power. In Africa and other parts of the world where witchcraft reigns, people live in fear of evil spirits and curses. Africans would no doubt see John's experience as a provoked attack, manipulated by an enemy. His testimony before the snakebite that God is all-powerful now carries the added proof of his own personal experience.

Three years later, as John and Wanne remember this experience, they declare, "We serve an amazing God!"

When Christ followers accept a call to serve Him in another country, they must put their trust fully in this awesome God. While it is easy on the heels of an experience like John's, it is more difficult when young missionaries are just starting out. To go far away from family and friends to an unknown country and learn a new language and way of life require great faith. The situation is compounded when children are involved.

Such was the case with Tim and Janice McCall when they went as missionaries to Africa in 1984. Their spirit of excitement in embarking on a new life in the Dark Continent was tempered somewhat by their concern for their four young children—for their health and safety, their education, their spiritual and emotional development. In these matters Tim and Janice put the children in their Father's hands. After all, did He not love them even more than they did?

The first year's adjustment on the missions field challenges any missionary. Learning a new language, accepting new customs, developing new tastes for food, and sometimes dealing with difficult work situations takes grit and grace. Tim and Janice were making great strides in adapting to their new home and place of service in Eku, Nigeria. Tim found working in the hospital both challenging and fulfilling, and Janice was learning to balance her many responsibilities as mother, wife, hostess, and spiritual advisor. Having four small children without K-Mart and McDonald's, to say nothing of *Sesame Street,* called for new talents and resources!

Just as they were beginning to breathe easy in their new home, a near tragedy tested their faith. Janice had just checked on David, their 5-year-old son, and found him playing quietly in his room. Suddenly, she was startled by his screams. She ran quickly to his room, with Tim close behind. Tim, fortunately, had finished at the hospital and had come home early. What they saw next sent chills down their spines. As they entered David's room, a small black snake slithered into the closet. Tim killed the snake, recognizing it as one of Africa's most deadly species.

As a doctor, Tim knew the first step was cut the wound to draw out the deadly venom and apply pressure above the bite. At the same time, he told Janice to run to the hospital for antivenom. When she returned minutes later, her face was ashen. "Tim, there is no antivenom at the hospital!"

What could they do? The nearest hospital, the Baptist Hospital at Ogbomosho, was located seven or eight hours away. Janice then suggested in desperation that she would fly David back to the United States, but Tim calmly told her that that attempt, too, would be impossible. All they could do was watch him through the night and keep him comfortable.

All throughout the night they kept a desperate and lonely vigil. It soon became evident that the deadly venom had entered the blood stream. Little David's fever rose rapidly; his leg swelled and turned a charcoal gray. At last Tim admitted to his wife that the situation did not look good. Only time and prayer would determine the outcome. At best, David could lose his foot and perhaps his leg. At worst, he could lose his very life.

Praying for her children had long since become a daily discipline for Janice. Once a week for years, she had fasted and prayed for them. This situation called for reinforcements, however. She ran quickly through the Mission compound, awaking her missionary colleagues, telling them of David's grave condition and asking them to watch and pray with them.

Soon the little missionary community, still in their nightclothes, began to rally around the family, encircling them with their presence and prayers of earnest petition. Even as the swelling continued to creep up David's leg, they continued to raise fervent prayers. By this time, David was delirious.

At daybreak those who had stood vigil for hours witnessed a miracle. The swelling in David's leg began to subside; his fever broke. Opening his eyes, he asked for water. This small response brought great thanksgiving in the hearts of those standing by. But the doctors, nurses, and family members whose lives had been wrapped up in medicine, knew the child was not yet out of the woods. He would live, but would he lose some part of his leg? Waiting and prayers continued. The prayers, however, soon turned from anxious petition to praise and thanksgiving.

Today David, a healthy college student at Baylor University in Texas, competes as an outstanding athlete with two strong legs. If you asked him, he might show you the two visible marks on his foot from the forked tongue of a snake. This scar, his parents have told him, remains as a reminder of the day God chose to spare his life and limb through the miraculous power of prayer.

WHEN SATAN'S FANGS HIT THEIR MARK

Reading of miraculous recoveries like these, we rejoice. Inside, however, a small voice says, "But what about the one who was not so fortunate, who lost his life from a snakebite? Did he not have enough faith? Were not enough people praying for him?"

You have likely prayed that a friend or loved one would survive a life-threatening condition, and thankfully, she lived. But perhaps you had the opposite answer to your prayer. In spite of the intercessory prayer of many faithful Christians your friend died. Did God not hear your prayer? Why does He answer our prayers on behalf of some but seem to turn deaf ears to our pleas for others? Do we worship a capricious God? Does He have favorites in the family?

Look again at the earlier reference to the sending out of the 70. Notice Jesus' response to their report: "'I watched Satan fall from heaven like a flash of lightning'" (Luke 10:18 NRSV).

In the victories they ascribed to Jesus, they were able to experience the ultimate fall of Satan. The miracles, not contrived, personal victories, were laid at the feet of a powerful Master. But Jesus warned, "'Nevertheless, do not rejoice at this, that the spirits submit to you, but rejoice that your names are written in heaven.'" Jesus noted the miracles, but He commended the relationship with God. More important than even the "beyond belief" experiences in our lives, we treasure the eternal life we know in Christ.

WHEN SNAKES BITE AND SCORPIONS STING

If you ask one of our Last Frontier missionaries why he or she goes to the ends of the earth, you are likely to be reminded of Jesus' words, "'The harvest is plentiful, but the laborers are few; therefore ask the Lord of the harvest to send out laborers into his harvest. Go on your way. See, I am sending you out like lambs into the midst of the wolves.'" And snakes. And scorpions.

Hubert Mitchell knew all about all these. Reared in a Christian environment, he and his wife, Helen, felt led to become missionaries to the unreached tribes of Sumatra, Indonesia. He experienced many life-changing miracles in his ministry to the Kubu people in the jungle and Muslims on the island of Banka, the most prominent of which involved a nail.

Early in his ministry Hubert witnessed to the Kubu chief, but he had difficulty explaining the suffering of Christ on the Cross because the tribe was so primitive it had no concept of a nail. One day Hubert opened a can of fruit and discovered a three-inch-long nail inside. Once the chief understood Christ's crucifixion, he accepted His salvation. As a result, Hubert began a physically arduous evangelistic ministry resulting in the salvation of hundreds of Kubus.

Mixed with the victories, Hubert experienced loss as well. His wife, Helen, weakened by attacks of malaria and other tropical maladies, died three days after the birth of their daughter in 1940.

While Bill and I were serving as missionaries on Java, Indonesia, we heard a song Hubert had written, and while never meeting him personally, felt a union with him as we performed his beautiful "He Giveth More Grace."[2]

He giveth more grace when the burdens grow
    greater;
He sendeth more strength when the labors
    increase.
To added affliction he addeth His mercy,
To multiplied trials, His multiplied peace.

When we have exhausted our store of endurance,
When our strength is gone e'er the day is half
    done,
When we've reached the end of our hoarded
    resources,
Our Father's full giving is only begun.

Refrain:
His love has no limit, His grace has no measure,
His power has no boundary known unto men.
For out of His infinite riches in Jesus
He giveth, and giveth, and giveth again.

If you live long enough, you will bear many scars. You may avoid snakes and scorpions, but we are all subject to life's tragedies. When they come your way, here are some remedies I have found helpful.

• Find solace in God's Word. Ask the Holy Spirit to guide you in the verses you need.

• Read the Psalms and other meaningful passages aloud. This has brought me unusual blessings. Singing hymns warms the heart, especially when your hurt is deep.

• Remember God is always ready to hear you. Come honestly before Him. He is able to hear your words of anger and resentment. Even if you come kicking and screaming, He loves you and meets you in your need.

• Know that deep hurt and sadness does not dissipate quickly. Be patient with yourself.

• Let others minister to you; but when you need to be alone, say so. Because I am fiercely independent, I do not want to presume on anyone's time. I made a new discovery! Your friends have a need to help. Let them.

• As soon as you are able, reach out to someone else in need. This is effective medicine in recovery.

• Remember that being a part of God's family entitles you to apply for His strength and confidence.

Pray that God will enable you to use your snakebite and scorpion stings in ministering to those who have similar tragedies. Pray also for His servants who serve in difficult places. Treasure the awesome relationship you have with Christ and share His love with others.

[1]See *Missions Mosaic*. To subscribe, call 1-800-968-7301 or visit the WMU Web site at www.wmu.com.
[2]"He Giveth More Grace." Copyright 1941. Renewed 1969 by Lillenas Publishing Company. All rights reserved. Used by permission.

9

God's Greatest Miracle

If you had to choose, what would you select as Jesus' greatest miracle? Turning the water to wine? Healing the leper? Raising people from the dead? Any one of these acts of our Lord qualifies as great, but one miracle stands out, superceding all the rest. You will find a clue in John 4:3–42.

GOD'S GREATEST MIRACLE

She sank wearily to the edge of the well and wiped her brow with her robe. Such a hot day! She wished she could come earlier in the day before the sun got so hot, but she had tried that before. The heat of the tempers of the other women and the fiery words they hurled at her were far more hurtful than the sun's rays. This was better, to come quietly in the middle of the day, without fear of insults and criticisms.

She had seen Him as she neared Jacob's well, a solitary figure sitting on the wall, apparently resting from a morning's walk. Now she took another look, trying not to be obvious. Where was He from? Probably from Judea, based on His looks. But what was He doing here? The Jews never came to Samaria. Too good, they think! They can't mix with the likes of us Samaritans.

The Samaritan woman was not quite sure why they were considered as "untouchables." Something about Samaritans being half-breeds—half Jewish and half pagan, they say. With a sigh, she arose, took her large water container, and began to draw water.

"Give Me a drink."

She looked up, startled, only to find He was indeed talking to her. She stood and gestured to herself as she addressed Him. "Me? You're asking for a drink from me? You're a man, a rabbi, apparently, and a Jew. How can you possibly be speaking to me, a Samaritan woman?"

She could not have known that He had come to Jacob's well just to speak with her. While Samaria was on the most direct road from Judea to Galilee, His ultimate destination, the preferred route directed a Jewish traveler to cross the Jordan and go up the eastern side of the river, thus avoiding Samaria altogether. Then one could recross the Jordan and enter Galilee. While it would take twice as long, it did keep Jewish travelers from associating with the hated Samaritans.

The disciples may have argued with Jesus when they saw He planned to take the more direct route, but Jesus simply said, "I have to pass through Samaria." Now it was clear that His business in Samaria had something to do with this woman.

"'If you knew the gift of God, and who it is saying to you, "Give me a drink," you would have asked him, and he would have given you living water.'"

She had to laugh at this man's impertinence. "Sir, you have no bucket, and the well is deep. . . . Are you greater than our ancestor Jacob, who gave us the well?'"

The man refused to react to her haughty response. Instead He patiently (and could it be lovingly?) countered, "'Everyone who drinks of this water will be thirsty again, but those who drink of the water that I will give them will never be thirsty.'" She started to interrupt, but He continued, "This water will become in them a spring gushing up to eternal life."

Is this some kind of joke? she thought. But what if, what if He did have such water? Never again would she have to come in the heat of the day to this place. "'Sir, give me this water, so that I may never be thirsty or have to keep coming here to draw water."

"'Go, call your husband, and come back.'"

"'I have no husband.'"

"'You are right in saying, "I have no husband"; for you have had five husbands, and the one you have now is not your husband.'"

Her face fell. Did even this stranger know about her miserable life? She had to change the subject; this one was too painful. "'I see you are a prophet. Our ancestors worshiped on this mountain, but you say that the place where people must worship is in Jerusalem.'"

"'Believe me,'" He said, "'the hour is coming when you will worship the Father neither on this mountain nor in Jerusalem. . . . But the hour is coming, and is now here, when the true worshipers will worship the Father in spirit and truth, for the Father seeks such as these to worship him. God is spirit, and those who worship him must worship in spirit and truth.'"

His words were difficult to understand. Spirit. And truth. Yet there was such magnetism in His eyes, she could not find it within herself to withdraw. She did, however, step back a bit and smiled to cover her embarrassment. "'I know that Messiah is coming' (who is called Christ). "When he comes, he will proclaim all things to us.'"

Jesus' next three simple words pierced her heart and struck her dumb. "'I am he.'" Did she hear His words correctly? "'The one who is speaking to you.'"

The sound of men's voices interrupted the silence. The apostles had been sent to buy food for their Rabbi and for themselves. When they got closer to the well and saw their Master speaking to a woman, and a Samaritan woman at that, they were astonished. How could He? But not a one voiced his thoughts. They pretended not to notice as the woman ran silently away, leaving her water pot behind.

The woman hastened her pace as she neared her city. When she tried to speak, her words came out in a breathless whisper. "Come," she urged. "Come." The astonished men and women gathered while she attempted to get her breath. What could possibly have happened? They had never seen her so animated. Normally, she withdrew from crowds and went about her solitary business. But today she seemed—different. Her face was radiant, her testimony engaging. What was she going to say?

"'Come and see a man who told me everything I have ever done! He cannot be the Messiah, can he?'"

"The Messiah? He said He is the Messiah? This I've got to see." The people were incredulous.

Jesus was just in the process of explaining to His apostles why He was no longer hungry ("'My food is to do the will of him who sent me. . . . The fields are ripe for harvest.'") when the large crowd arrived at the well. Their response was staggering. Men and women, boys and girls came to know the gospel all because of the testimony of a woman considered unclean by fellow townspeople but now embraced by a loving Savior. During the following days Jesus stayed with these Samaritans and taught them lessons of grace and mercy.

"'It is no longer because of what you said that we believe, for we have heard for ourselves, and we know that this is truly the Savior of the world.'" Of all the many miraculous works of Jesus, salvation is undeniably the greatest. He loved this sinful, forgotten woman with an everlasting love. No one, regardless of his or her sin and imperfections, is out of the reach of God's grace. God's greatest miracle!

THE MIRACLE CONTINUES TODAY

In Indonesia

Following the attempted Communist coup d'état in Indonesia in 1965, the churches began to fill. Not only did Christians feel they could now gather safely together for worship, but also new faces began to appear in the congregations. The government of this Muslim country was unwilling to let godless Communism prevail. The Indonesian Army had led in a bloody countercoup in which hundreds of thousands were killed, and in the end, the government banned Communism altogether. In addition, the government leaders ruled that everyone must have a religion; no longer would they allow the atheism fostered by the Communist Party. A man or woman could choose to be Muslim, Hindu, Confucianist, Christian, or Catholic, but they must embrace a religious belief.

What an opportunity for the churches! Those who had been duped by the Communist leaders were searching for truth, and many found their way into our churches. Warm and fervent worship services attracted the lost, and many came to know Jesus as their Savior. At the close of one revival service in a church in our area, a man broke down and cried as though his heart would break. Christians gathered around him to try to give comfort, but the man was so emotional he could not reveal the source of his grief.

Finally, he regained his composure enough to say, "I want to have Jesus in my heart and life, but He could never receive me. My life is so full of sin." The Christians assured him that Jesus would forgive him of all his sins. But he cried all the more, "You can't know how evil I am. My hands are red with the blood of countless men. I'm a murderer! Jesus could never forgive me." He confessed his involvement in the deaths of many in the bloody coup. Someone brought out a Bible and read verses of assurance like:

"The blood of Jesus his Son cleanses us from all sin" (1 John 1:7 NRSV).

"He himself bore our sins in his body on the cross, so that, free from sins, we might live for righteousness" (1 Peter 2:24 NRSV).

"For I will forgive their iniquity, and remember their sin no more" (Jer. 31:34 NRSV).

Oh, the joy that flooded his heart! His sins were removed as far as the east is from the west. Islam offers no forgiveness as that found in Christianity. Repentance that results in absolute obliteration of guilt is unknown. Only in Christ are we granted full pardon, and only in Him are we entitled to membership in His family, regardless of the nature of our past lives.

112

In Georgia

Some would say Rose never had a chance. She grew up in a home where alcohol was a daily fact of life, and her mother and sister died from alcohol-related illnesses while Rose was still a teenager. At age 14 she was married and had a baby. By age 19, she had had her second child, was addicted to alcohol, had fallen in with the wrong crowd, and was ready to divorce her husband. Her father suggested she move far away in order to get a fresh start.

Rose's life seemed to be changing for the better when she settled in Needham, Massachusetts. After being trained at the Opportunity Industrial Center, a job-training program, she interviewed and was hired to work in the personnel office of GTE Sylvania. She was the first African American hired for work other than on the assembly line. Everything appeared finally to be going her way, except that her daughter, attending school in south Boston, was caught up in the civil rights riots. Then Rose received word that her grandmother, who had reared her, was dying of cancer, and she felt she needed to care for her. She returned to Augusta, Georgia, in September 1975, and her grandmother died two months later.

Rose again picked up her life. This time she enrolled in college and was eventually hired by a real estate company. For a number of years she had been drinking, and when she married her second husband in Boston, he introduced her to marijuana. In spite of this, she performed well at the real estate company, and when it was sold to the housing authority, she moved into a management position, which she held successfully for 21 years.

In the meantime, her children had grown up, each becoming involved in their own addictions and marital problems. Her son was arrested for stealing, and when he got out of prison he was still dependent upon drugs. When Rose began to date one of his friends who got her hooked on crack, her son suddenly became very protective of her. He moved in with her to protect her, to keep her away from an influence he did not like. One late night he became involved in an altercation with Rose's suitor, and the man stabbed Rose's son to death. It was almost more than Rose could bear. Five others close to her died within a five-month period as well. She lost her job. Not understanding why God would let these things happen to her, she just gave up.

One afternoon, while ironing clothes, she happened to see a new Bible lying on the table. When she opened the cover, she read, "Accepted Christ as my Lord and Savior, November 24, 1997." Rose realized her son had met the Lord Jesus just three months before his death. She was forced, however, to admit that she had never had a relationship with Jesus.

By this time Rose was serving as house manager with Heart Ministries, a shelter for battered women in Lavonia, Georgia, a Christian home for chemically dependent women. One evening as she drove the residents home in the van, she heard an almost audible voice saying, "You can let go now," and it seemed a peace overwhelmed her. She went to the cemetery, knelt at her son's grave, and released him. She thanked God for allowing her to have him for 36 years. Now she felt free of the guilt for his death. She experienced a new relationship with Christ.

Today Rose lives a happy, fulfilled life. She has had no desire to drink or use drugs since working with Heart Ministries and constantly praises God for delivering her from a life of sin and dependency.

In Nigeria

God rescues us not only out of a life of sin and chaos, but also out of pain and grief. His power is operative in every situation of life.

In 1990 Marjorie McCullough, then national president of WMU, and I visited several countries in West Africa. Bill Bullington of the Foreign Mission Board (now International Mission Board) and his wife, Evelyn, served as our tour guides. Marjorie was the perfect companion on such a trip, since she was a missionary to Nigeria years before. For her, it was a moving homecoming. For me, it was a dream come true. Since GA days I had heard about missionaries and their work in that part of the world. One place in particular held special interest. Ogbomosho, Nigeria, home not only of the seminary and many churches, was also the site for the Kersey Nutritional Clinic, a large hospital, many churches, and a leprosarium. I wanted to see it all! And the missionaries made it possible. The hospital provides medical services to that area, but seeks also to foster spiritual wellness through its evangelistic outreach. The seminary trains national pastors in their ministry to the churches. Mothers at the Kersey Home are in temporary residence with their children to learn more about the nutritional food they can both grow and prepare to provide for their children.

On Sunday morning we visited Promised Land, the home of many lepers and their families. Modern medical assistance has given them hope, and giant strides are being made, but not before many of them lose limbs. As we walked through the neighborhood, many were leaving their little huts, headed toward the little Baptist church that serves that area. We joined them in their destination.

While the service was similar in many ways to ours here in the US, we found some components quite unique. An RA opened the service with a dramatic drill into the simple church building. Because I could not understand the local language, the missionary provided translation, but one element needed no translation. At the appropriate time, the music director took his place before the congregation, but not by the means to which we are accustomed. He did not stand up, for he had no legs. Instead, he used a handmade skateboard attached to the stubs of his legs to maneuver to the front. He lifted hands, hands without fingers, to direct our singing. Most amazing, however, his face fairly glowed with the glorious happiness within. It truly reflected the description of God in Revelation 1:16 (NRSV), "And his face was like the sun shining with full force."

We had a similar experience when we were in Indonesia. Bill had taken a number of seminary students to a leprosarium operated by the government, located in a remote area. The patients quickly gathered around them, for no outsider had visited them in years. The seminary students had received orientation from a doctor in preparation for this ministry trip. They had been told that leprosy could not be passed on by simple contact, but no one could deny the test of courage and willingness necessary to risk for a spiritual ministry. One by one, they paired off, witnessing through the power of the touch and personal attention.

Later they gathered together for a service. The seminary choir sang, the first music of this kind that many of these forgotten ones had heard. The student designated "preacher of the day" began his message, when one of the men interrupted, "I want to sing for you." His body appeared to be wasted away, his appendages ravaged by the ancient disease. He wore shorts and a simple shirt, his open wounds dressed in rags, but he could not have been more gloriously arrayed had he worn the world's most expensive tuxedo.

His eyes fixed on a vision visible only to him; his voice was raised to his God. The seminary students were amazed. In perfect English he sang his first hymn. When he finished that song, he announced his intention to sing again. This time, he brought tears to every eye as he sang:

The great Physician now is near,
The sympathizing Jesus;
He speaks the drooping heart to cheer,
Oh! hear the voice of Jesus.

Your many sins are all forgiv'n,
Oh! hear the voice of Jesus;
Go on your way in peace to heav'n,
And wear a crown with Jesus.

Refrain:
Sweetest note in seraph song,
Sweetest name on mortal tongue;
Sweetest carol ever sung,
Jesus, blessed Jesus.

Where had he learned that hymn? More importantly, where had he heard the glorious message of this Great Physician? Yet, here he stood in a remote area of the island of Java, Indonesia, giving acknowledgement to his hope in Christ. The awesome power of God is operative into the far reaches of the world.

The woman at the well, living a life of sin and ostracism.

The guerilla with blood on his hands.
Rose, bound up in a destructive lifestyle.
Those marked by leprosy.

What do they have in common? The touch of a Savior Who loves them and has saved them from past sins and illnesses to a glorious future with Him. This greatest of all miracles is available to anyone who will receive it.

TREASURES IN CLAY JARS

Second Corinthians 4:7 (NRSV) sums it all up: "We have this treasure in clay jars, so that it may be made clear that this extraordinary power belongs to God and does not come from us."

Perhaps you have been saved from an unusually sordid or miserable past. You know God's power to forgive sins in a unique way. Those who have never been on drugs, never even thought of killing someone, should remember that we, too, were outside God's love and forgiveness until He intervened and brought new life to our souls. Salvation is truly God's greatest miracle.

Do you spend time each day thanking God for His great gift to you? John wrote these words in his Gospel: "To all who received him, who believed in his name, he gave power to become children of God, who were born, not of blood or of the will of the flesh or of the will of man, but of God'" (John 1:12–13 NRSV).

The gift giving cannot be complete until we pass it on to someone else. Ask God to give you the opportunity to do just that. Ask Him to point you to someone who needs this miracle. Pray for the courage and the love of Jesus in order to pass the message to her, regardless of the emotional and traditional distance you might feel. It may be that the one who needs it most lives outside the orbit of your daily life. It may also be true that someone you work with or casually know may never hear the gospel anywhere else but from you. The ball is in your court. Go and tell her this awesome Savior loves her and died for her. It will bring joy beyond belief.

Seed of the Church

People in every age seek heroes. In the closing days of the 1900s, magazine publishers and organizations named the "century's best" in numerous categories and even placed their nominations for "most signifi-cant" person of the millennium. The lists included the familiar names of government leaders, outstand-ing athletes, great artists, noted authors, civil rights leaders, and others.

Many critics of today say either our generation has no heroes, or that the heroes we uphold do not project an image worthy of emulation. Some even say we do our best to tear down the image of our leaders.

Webster-Merriam's Collegiate Dictionary, 10th ed., defines a hero as, "A man (and the feminine *heroine,* a woman) admired for his achievements and noble qualities; one that shows great courage; the central figure in an event, period, or movement."

How would you define a hero? Certainly we admire a person for his or her talent, fame, or courage. We might aspire to be like that person, if it just didn't cost so much in dedication.

RISK IN THE EARLY CHURCH
Some people become heroes by great sacrifice, even martyrdom. These individuals are so committed to a

person or a cause that they will pay whatever it takes in a test of devotion, even if it is the ultimate price.

The Chinese word for *crisis* is comprised of two pictographs for danger and opportunity. These two words clearly characterize the situation in the Jerusalem church after Christ's death. To preach the message of One Who had just been crucified for claiming to be the Messiah was certain to entail danger. The religious leaders would be watching His followers very carefully to avoid any possibility of their propagating such lies. And yet the disciples had to admit they had an overwhelming opportunity to take advantage of the great interest generated by Jesus' recent death and resurrection and the incredible circumstances surrounding it. Should they be careful about being too overt with the gospel, or should they take advantage of their remarkable opportunity and shout it from the rooftops?

The decision was made for them on Pentecost (Acts 2). The Holy Spirit fell upon Christ's closest followers, and His power thrust them out of the upper room, directly into the presence of the most diverse gathering one could imagine—Parthians, Medes, and Elamites; residents of Mesopotamia, Judea, and Cappadocia; visitors from Rome; and on and on. Amazingly, each ethnic group heard the message in its own language. Peter presented the message of God powerfully, and on that day 3,000 people believed and were baptized. Imagine trying to assimilate 3,000 members into your church membership in one week!

In the next days and weeks the apostles performed many wonders and signs through the power of God's Spirit, and the church gathered often for fellowship and praising God. An ever-increasing number of people were added to the church. The new believers marveled at the healing of the sick.

The Jewish leaders, however, noted the growing strength of the church with both fear and anger. The high priest ordered the arrest of the apostles, but even the prison could not hold them. An angel opened the doors and brought them out, saying, "'Go, stand in the temple and tell the people the whole message about life" (Acts 5:17–20 NRSV).

When the council of the high priest, debating their decision for punishment, heard that the apostles had been miraculously set free, and furthermore were even then preaching Christ in the temple, they knew the situation was desperate. To deal severely with the apostles could result in a negative reaction from the people, yet they could not let it go. Just at the height of their furor, the rational appeal from one of their own, the highly respected Gamaliel, somewhat cooled their desire for blood. Generally, he advised, "Let's be reasonable about this. We have precedents in others who in the past have claimed to be someone special and in each case their threat has died out in its own time. Just let these men be, and if their movement is not of God it, too, will die. However, if it is of God, you will not be able to overthrow them" (Acts 5:33–39).

Gamaliel's wisdom prevailed, and the apostles were beaten and then released. The apostles, however, wore this persecution as a badge of courage and continued in their evangelistic efforts. Rather than fearing for their lives, they rejoiced that they were counted worthy to suffer dishonor for Jesus' sake (Acts 5:34–42). Instead of backing down, they prayed for more courage in declaring the works of Christ (Acts 4:29–30).

But the hero of this story is not Peter or Paul or any other of the apostles, although they were instrumental in setting the stage. Their courage simply inspired another in "beyond belief" commitment. Stephen, whose name means "wreath" or "crown," had taken his place among the redeemed of the Lord. Although not a Greek himself, he, like many others, spoke Greek and was called a Hellenist. Among this group within the church were those who perceived that the needs of their poor, especially those of the widows, were not being met. When the apostles became aware of the problem, they did what we often do today in our churches: they formed a committee and told the Hellenists to choose seven men, full of the Spirit and wisdom, to fill it. Stephen was the first one chosen by his peers. In keeping with his continued spiritual growth, the power of God's Spirit enabled him to work great signs and miracles. As his influence among the church grew, the Jews frequently singled him out in open argument. Because of Stephen's wisdom and the power of the Spirit working within him, they lost every debate (Acts 6–7).

Finally, the Jews had only one weapon left in their arsenal: a false witness who would declare that Stephen had spoken blasphemous words against both Moses and God. This false testimony, so persuasively given, made condemnation almost certain. The Christians standing by anxiously awaited Stephen's defense. To their surprise they detected no fear in his eyes. As a matter of fact, Stephen's face was like the face of an angel!

Stephen began with the beginning of the story, with Abraham, Isaac, and Jacob. He told again the familiar story of their heroic Moses leading the people into the Promised Land and of the building of the Temple in Jerusalem.

Suddenly Stephen departed from the historic account. In essence he accused, "But through it all the people never knew our God, never met His expectations. You are a stiff-necked people, just like your ancestors were. They rejected the prophets who foretold the coming of the Messiah; now you have rejected the Son of God himself" (Acts 7:51–53). That was all it took. The people were enraged and ground their teeth at him. Stephen himself, however, remained calm, in fact serene; for he looked up and was blessed with a vision of "the glory of God and Jesus standing at the right hand of God" (v. 55 NRSV). When the mob, with blood in their eyes, had carried Stephen to a place outside the city, he knew their intent. He watched as they took off their coats, lifted huge stones, and felt the piercing of the first blows.

"Lord Jesus, receive my spirit." As modeled by Jesus on His cross, Stephen's last words reflected his Master's grace and mercy, "'Lord, do not hold this sin against them'" (v. 60 NRSV).

"The witnesses laid their coats at the feet of a young man named Saul. . . . And Saul approved of their killing him" (Acts 7:58 to 8:1): a little noticed detail in the murderous scenario; a tremendous motivating factor in the church's history. Stephen's death signaled the beginning of an era of persecution of Christians and expansion of the church. Rather than destroy Christianity, persecution would only strengthen it. Tertullian wrote in the last half of the second century: "We multiply wherever we are mown down by you; the blood of Christians is seed." In *Fox's Book of Martyrs* we find, "This persecution was general throughout the whole Roman Empire; but it rather increased than diminished the spirit of Christianity."[1]

In the second century's persecutions in Africa, Perpetua, a young wife of 22 years of age, and her friend, Felicitas, pregnant and nearing her due date, were imprisoned. Only days after Felicitas gave birth to her child, the two women were taken to the amphitheater, stripped, and thrown to a mad bull. The executioner completed what the bull so horribly began.[2] It is difficult to understand man's inhumanity to man, but the courage of the martyrs is beyond belief.

MARTYRS TODAY?

Do you as a Christian feel persecuted for your faith? True, we often speak of the difficulty of being a Christian today, but while we Americans may occasionally be harassed and discriminated against because of our faith, we hardly know the meaning of persecution. The shootings at Columbine High School and Fort Worth's Wedgwood Baptist Church brought grief and fear to the Christian community and in some instances might be considered persecution. As despicable as those events were, however, we must be careful not to equate them with the wholesale horrors encountered by the faithful followers of Christ in other lands who face arrest, torture, and even death solely for their belief.

Chances are no one reading this book has ever been called upon to risk his life for the sake of the gospel. We are fortunate to live in a land where its people are granted the right to worship, or not worship, as they please. Our Constitution established that freedom from the beginning. However, more Christians have been martyred throughout the world in this century than all the other 1,900 years combined.

In the year 1999 alone, with 33.1 percent of the world's population declaring themselves to be Christians, approximately 164,000 have been killed rather than renounce their faith in Christ, more than four times those martyred in 1900! By the year 2025 it is projected that there will be 210,000 Christian martyrs due to accelerated missionary activity and an increasingly hostile world.[3]

The Birmingham News on February 24, 2000, carried the news of a deadly religious clash in Nigeria. "Charred bodies and burned-out cars littered the streets of the north central city of Kaduna. . . . An overwhelming stench filled the morgue at the main hospital, where dozens of bodies were piled up on slabs, on the floor, and even on the ground outside." The report indicated that some 200 were killed. At least 6 of the dead were associated with the Baptist seminary in Kaduna, which on Tuesday, February 22, was burned to the ground. The riot erupted in connection with a peaceful demonstration by Christians against a proposal to bring Islamic law to Kaduna State. While minor clashes have occurred in Nigeria in the past, this recent attack raises new concerns for the peaceful coexistence of Christians and Muslims in this major African nation.

In just more than 60 countries, according to an official US State Department report in 1997, "Christians face the reality of massacre, rape, torture, mutilation, family division, harassment, imprisonment, slavery, discrimination in education and employment, and even death."[4] Why are Christians so often persecuted, especially in the Third World? Paul Marshall in *Their Blood Cries Out* says: "Their usually peaceful and quiet beliefs stand as a rebuke to those that are corrupt, to those who cannot tolerate the presence of any view but their own, and to those who want to make their own political regime the only focus of loyalty."[5] Persecuted Christians are mostly women, because the Church's membership is disproportionately female, according to Marshall.[6]

One such woman, May Hayman, was born in 1905, in Australia. The sixth child in a family of eight, she trained as a nurse and then served with the Anglican New Guinea missionary staff from 1936 until her death in 1942.

May's friendly, generous spirit matched well the simple natives of New Guinea. In 1942, however, the Japanese interrupted her work among them. In July of that year, they bombarded the Gona Mission where May was working. She and another nurse escaped briefly to the jungle bush but were betrayed by hostile natives who delivered them over to the Japanese. The two of them were murdered on August 11, 1942, and were buried in a trench at a coffee plantation.[7]

JIHAD IN INDONESIA

Martyrdom seems especially despicable when it involves youth. Their deaths are often said to be accidents, "being in the wrong place at the wrong time" when atrocities occur. Children have sometimes lost their lives in the burning of churches and church schools in Nigeria and Indonesia, for example. But often, youth receive intentional focus. Such was the case with Roy in 1999.

Roy was a simple, fun-loving, 15-year-old boy living on Ambon, an island in eastern Indonesia. Ambon is one of the Moluccas, in the Bandea Sea. (The Moluccas are also known as the Spice Islands, the destination of Columbus's three ships when he discovered America instead. Imagine how history would have changed if he had been successful in his initial quest!)

Roy loved to play *sepak bola,* Indonesian football, similar to our soccer. He sometimes helped in the rice field and tended to his four younger siblings, carrying the youngest in a long piece of Indonesian batik. In the heat of the day, he often cut a piece of sugar cane fresh from the field and felt the sweet, sticky syrup on his face.

When school was in session, his schedule changed drastically because Roy took his studies in the third level of junior high seriously. All year around, everyone in his small fishing community knew that he could be found at his church on the Lord's Day because he was a faithful Christian and member of King's Kids.

Roy is not typical of most boys and girls in Indonesia because almost 90 percent of the population in this fourth most populous country in the world is Islamic. Christians make up just less than 10 percent. The Portuguese, the first Europeans to reach Ambon, established a fort there and began trading for spices in 1512. Since that time, Christianity has become the major religion of the area. The Dutch captured the fort in 1605, and except for a 3-year period when the British and Japanese occupied Ambon, it was held by the Dutch until 1949, when Indonesia won its independence. Ambon led a brief revolt against Indonesia in 1950 in a bid to secede; but since that time, they have maintained a shaky, relative peace. When clashes have occurred between Christians and Muslims, they most often happen in conjunction with a holy day.

But back to Roy. He had long been anticipating the month of January 1999 because some 120 members of his church were going to a retreat at Hila Beach near Ambon. For the church members, the site was special because the Portuguese built the very first church there in 1580. Although it had subsequently been burned down, Christians hold this oldest church with pride.

The day before the retreat ended, January 19, 1999, Muslims entered the second day of Idulfitri, the month of fast preceding the Islamic new year. One of the Christian pastors, along with a hired driver, had left for a nearby village to find a larger vehicle to return his members to their homes following the retreat. News had not come to Hila that the pastor and his driver never reached their destination. Assailants had killed the men by throwing kerosene on the interior of the car and setting it on fire.

The next day those attending the retreat, with the program having ended, were preparing to leave when they heard a truck entering the fishing complex. The passengers, residents of the neighboring Muslim village, waved machetes and other weapons and shouted heated threats. The Christians sought protection in the nearest building, but they were quickly forced into the open area. Some of the teenagers and children ran to the water, swam to the opposite side, and escaped into the woods.

Roy, however, was grabbed by one of the assailants. "Hey, young man. Not so fast." As he began to ridicule him and the Lord he loved, Roy struggled to get away. This enraged the man even more, and he pointed his machete at him.

"Now, young man, I'll give you a chance to save yourself. Denounce your God and give service to Muhammad, the great prophet. Denounce your faith in this Jesus. Say it, now!" Roy's friends and his 9-year-old brother stood silently by, praying for the Lord to work a miracle to save Roy's life.

The seconds that followed the order seemed interminable; the air, only moments before full of joy, was now leaden. Suddenly, Roy said with a loud voice, "I am Christ's soldier!" clutching his Bible close to his chest to strengthen his vow. Then the crowd was horrified to see the man swing the machete, releasing the Bible and dismembering Roy's arm from his body.

"Again, boy. One more chance. Denounce this Jesus."

But Roy once again bravely stated, "I am Christ's soldier." This time the machete found its mark, severing Roy's other arm. And again, when he refused to deny his Lord, Roy unmercifully received the final, deathblow. His body was thrown into a ditch from which it was retrieved days later and returned to his home village for simple ceremonies in the middle of the night.

On January 23, 2000, Moluccan Christians in Britain, Holland, and other parts of the world made an appeal to the worldwide Christian community to join them in prayer for the persecuted in the Spice Islands. Churches have been burned and approximately 2,000 Christians and Muslims have been killed in this year. Wilfred Wong, parliamentary officer for the Jubilee Campaign, an interdenominational Christian human rights pressure group, has said, "The Moluccas is one of the few areas in the world today where so many Christians are being slaughtered on such a frequent basis because of their faith."[8] Christians are called to pray for sectarian violence in every area of the world.

We are not told what effect the courage of a young man from a small fishing village had on his murderers. No doubt, some felt justified in their acts. After all, it was only one isolated event in the jihad, the Islamic holy war. Could the boldness, the commitment of one young man to his faith, produce fertile soil for the work of the Holy Spirit in the heart of someone who witnessed it? Did this tragedy linger in his heart and mind so that he, like Paul, would one day say: "I am grateful to Christ Jesus our Lord, who has strengthened me, because he judged me faithful and appointed me to his service, even though I was formerly a blasphemer, a persecutor, and a man of violence. But I received mercy because I had acted ignorantly in unbelief, and the grace of our Lord overflowed for me with the faith and love that are in Christ Jesus. The saying is sure and worthy of full acceptance, that Christ Jesus came into the world to save sinners—of whom I am the foremost" (1 Tim. 1:12–15 NRSV).

Hostilities have spilled over into the Indonesian island of Lombok, when a rally was held by Muslims to protest the events in Ambon. The number of Christians on this island is small, only about 1 percent of the population. CNN (CNN.com) reported that when the rally turned violent, Muslims burned at least ten churches and attacked Christians. No doubt, being a faithful Christian in some plces in today's world requires an incredible amount of faith and courage.

Stephen's martyrdom was only the first of countless men, women, and children who have made the supreme sacrifice for their Lord. In our country where people are free to worship as we choose, we can hardly imagine such a great sacrifice for our belief. Would I be willing to openly and courageously proclaim allegiance to God with a knife to my neck? If the day ever came that we paid dearly for what we now so often take for granted, would we be faithful?

Jesus warned His followers that tension would sometimes bring personal harm, discrimination, even death. "'Remember the word that I said to you, "Servants are not greater than their master." If they persecuted me, they will persecute you'" (John 15:20 NRSV). How much are you willing to risk for Christ?

An active church member was discussing her church's upcoming missions trip in a rather unsettled part of the world. "But I'm sure the church wouldn't send us if it weren't safe." Really? If not us, then who?

Now let's be practical. What can we do to help persecuted Christians? How can we help to bear their burdens? First of all, we can be aware. Too often we have chosen to keep our heads in the ground about this matter. Make it a point to educate yourself about the extent of persecution today.

Second, support legislation that takes action against regimes that deprive citizens of their religious freedoms. Know the names of your elected officials and don't hesitate to bring incidents of religious oppression to their attention.

Third, and most important, pray. Thank God for the faithful witness of persecuted believers. Pray for their families, often left without support. Pray for the repentance and salvation of oppressors. Pray for believers in Communist and Islamic countries. Pray that government leaders of democratic countries will have the courage to speak out against the violation of human rights. Pray that Westerners will be stirred to action and that they will no longer tolerate the religious persecution in many parts of our world.

When Stephen faced his oppressors, he prayed for them. Unbelievable mercy and grace! It was when he was willing to give his all that he was most like Christ. His death unleashed the power of a germinating seed, and great was the harvest therefrom!

[1]William Byron Forbush, ed., *Fox's Book of Martyrs* (Grand Rapids, MI: Zondervan Publishing House, 1967), 6.

[2]Ibid., 13.

[3]David B. Barrett and Todd M. Johnson, "Annual Statistical Table on Global Mission: 1999," *International Bulletin of Missionary Research*, January 1999, 25.

[4]Shatter the Silence! (www.persecutedchurch.org).

[5]Paul Marshall, *Their Blood Cries Out* (Waco, TX: Word Publishing, 1997), 9.

[6]Ibid., 8.

[7]*Beeson Divinity Chapel*, n.p., n.d.

[8]Jubilee Campaign (info@jubileecampaign.demon.co.uk).

Epilogue

When I began to write this book, I did as I always attack any assignment—I got organized. First I wrote the proposal, the plan for the book. I wrote the tentative chapter headings, the proposed contents, and even a prologue. Then I thought I was set to begin. Silly me! First of all, the "I's" had to be eliminated. That was easy, for the Holy Spirit kept taking the book away from me. Chapter titles, even content, drastically changed. God kept bringing people who shared stories that simply had to be told. Memories buried away in my memory were nudged to consciousness and to a place in this book.

What I expected to be a chore, the writing of this book, was instead one of life's great blessings. So many events remind us of God's miracles in our lives, if we just open our spiritual eyes and acknowledge His work. Many more volumes could be written.

I acknowledge two hopes in this book. First, I hope that I have complied with WMU's request for a book on our emphasis, Beyond Belief. Secondly, and most importantly, I pray that I have been a faithful conduit for the Holy Spirit's testimonies to God's power. As my son-in-law is prone to say, "I hope it knocks your socks off!" Maybe a little more spiritual expression is found in Revelation 19:6: "'Hallelujah! Salvation and glory and power belong to our God.'"

DELLANNA W. O'BRIEN
FEBRUARY 2000

About the author
Dellanna W. O'Brien served as executive director/treasurer of Woman's Missionary Union, Auxiliary to Southern Baptist Convention from September 1989 to September 1999. Previously she was president of International Family and Children's Educational Services in Richmond, Virginia. She also served with her husband, Bill, as a missionary to Indonesia. She holds degrees from Hardin-Simmons University and Texas Christian University and earned a doctorate in education from Virginia Tech and State University. She has also received several honorary doctorate degrees. The O'Briens have three adult children and six grandchildren. They make their home in Birmingham, Alabama.

If you enjoyed this book, you will also enjoy *Russian Harvest, China Bound, Follow the Call,* and *Transformed: Shaped by the Hand of God.*

Available by calling WMU Customer Service at 1-800-968-7301, and by visiting the WMU Web site at www.wmu.com.

Watch for *Beyond Belief, vol. 2,* by Barbara Joiner, available spring 2001.